215

Onderzoek en beleid

Prevention of Organised Crime

A situational approach

Henk van de Bunt

Cathelijne van der Schoot

BJu | Boom Juridische uitgevers

Justitie

Wetenschappelijk Onderzoek- en
Documentatiecentrum

Onderzoek en beleid

De reeks Onderzoek en beleid omvat de rapporten van door het WODC van het
Ministerie van Justitie verricht onderzoek.
Opname in de reeks betekent niet dat de inhoud van de rapporten het standpunt
van de Minister van Justitie weergeeft.

Exemplaren van dit rapport kunnen worden besteld bij het distributiecentrum
van Boom Juridische uitgevers.
Copies of this report can be ordered at the distribution centre of Boom
Juridische uitgevers:
Boom distributiecentrum, Pb. 400, 7940 AK Meppel
Tel. 0522-23 75 55
Fax 0522-25 38 64
E-mail bdc@bdc.boom.nl

Voor ambtenaren van het Ministerie van Justitie is een beperkt aantal gratis
exemplaren beschikbaar.
Deze kunnen worden besteld bij:
Bibliotheek WODC, kamer KO 14
Postbus 20301, 2500 EH Den Haag
Deze gratis levering geldt echter slechts zolang de voorraad strekt.

De integrale tekst van de WODC-rapporten is gratis te downloaden van
www.wodc.nl.
Op www.wodc.nl is ook nadere informatie te vinden over andere WODC-
publicaties.

ISBN 90-5454-425-2

Acknowledgements

This project was financed by the European Commission's Falcone programme. In 2000, the Research and Documentation Centre of the Ministry of Justice in the Netherlands (WODC) and Europol submitted an application for a research project on 'The identification and prevention of opportunities that facilitate organised crime'. The purpose of the research project was to explore the possibilities of preventing organised crime, in cooperation with three other research institutes in Italy, Finland and Hungary. Criminal case studies would provide the basis for identifying the possibilities for crime prevention.

The project has resulted in four national reports, containing as many as 60 case studies from Italy, Finland, Hungary and the Netherlands, and a final report. Due to a number of circumstances, the completion of the final report was delayed. At the end of 2002, the WODC requested the Departments of Criminology at Erasmus University Rotterdam and the Vrije Universiteit of Amsterdam to complete the Dutch national report (by translating and finishing the Dutch case studies) and to write the final report. After the acceptance of the assignment, researchers in the Departments of Criminology at Erasmus University Rotterdam and the Vrije Universiteit of Amsterdam commenced their activities in early 2003. The final report is the product of the joint effort of several researchers.

In this final report, the examples and insights of the four national reports from Finland, Hungary, Italy and The Netherlands were used as a blueprint. Due to the confidential nature of the national reports, their contents will not be made public. The national reports have been sent to the WODC, who bears the final overall responsibility for this project.

Many institutions and researchers have contributed to this project. First of all, we would like to thank the European Commission for financing this project. Jean Jacques Nuss, Directorates-General Justice and Home Affairs, guided this project on behalf of the European Commission. We would also like to thank UNICRI, Europol, and in particular the researchers who were involved in preparing the national reports of Italy, Finland and Hungary:

- Transcrime (Research Centre on Transnational Crime), University of Trento, Italy: Andrea di Nicola and Eleonora Garosi under the supervision of Prof. Ernesto Savona;
- National Bureau of Investigation (Keskusrikospoliisi), Helsinki, Finland: Harri Korpisaari and Tuija Hietaniemi;
- Institute of Criminology (OKRI), Budapest, Hungary: Tünde Barábas under the supervision of Ferenc Irk.

The Dutch national report was written by Cathelijne van der Schoot (Erasmus University Rotterdam) under the supervision of Prof. Henk van de Bunt. At an earlier stage, Marion Brienen, Charlotte van der Meij and Bartheke Docter-Schamhardt (WODC) were involved in preparing the case studies.

We would especially like to acknowledge the contributions of Prof. Henk van de Bunt and his colleagues Cathelijne van der Schoot, Hans Nelen, Francien Lankhorst, Wim Huisman, Aljen van Dijken, Peter Klerks and Jurjen Boorsma. The final report was drawn up promptly and professionally. Furthermore, we would like to thank Prof. Ronald Clarke (Rutgers University) who acted as general consultant, as well as Edward Kleemans and Jan Rademaker (WODC).

We would like to express the hope that the findings of this project will contribute to the further development of research on the prevention of organised crime and that the results of our study can be put into practice.

Prof. F.L. Leeuw
Director WODC

Table of contents

Summary

This final report is part of the Falcone project entitled 'The Identification and Prevention of Opportunities that Facilitate Organised Crime'. Four participating countries, namely Finland, Hungary, Italy and the Netherlands, have each drawn up a report in which 15 cases of organised crime are described and analysed. These descriptions are based on data from police files. The goal of this analysis is to reveal the interfaces between the legitimate and illegitimate environments and to generate possibilities for preventive action. These indications for possible preventive interventions are called 'red flags'. This final report comprises these 'red flags' from the four national reports and examines four selected topics in more depth: the role of public administration and local businesses, the legal professions, official and informal financial services, and forged official documents.

The preventive approach is not primarily aimed at the perpetrators of organised crime, but rather at the facilitating circumstances of organised crime. It addresses governments, civilians and enterprises and is an attempt to make them feel responsible for the prevention of organised crime. The message is actually quite simple: if criminal organisations are able to easily acquire or access resources, then the number of these resources have to be reduced, or made more difficult to acquire or access.

The findings of the national reports

The national reports identified various interfaces between organised crime groups and the legitimate environment, which are of vital importance to the existence organised crime. These contacts or 'red flags' are a threat to the legitimate environment, but they also offer opportunities for organised crime prevention. The interfaces identified in the national reports could be divided into three categories: the demand for illegal products and services from the licit environment, the abuse of facilitators in the licit environment and the availability of 'tools' in the licit environment. Three categories of preventive measures could thus be identified. The three categories will be briefly explained and illustrated with an example.

Firstly, the demand from the licit environment for illegal products and services forms a breeding ground for organised crime groups. A category of preventive measures is therefore aimed at reducing this demand. Here, it involves social and economic measures. After all, what is more effective than improving people's social conditions to prevent them from becoming involved in human smuggling, women trafficking and drug abuse? It is also possible to influence demand through legislation. The Dutch 'Benefit Entitlement (Residence Status) Act' (*Koppelingswet*) links social welfare to a person's residence permit which prevents illegal residence and the demand for illegal labour, which in turn influences the demand for human trafficking.

'Facilitators', persons whose knowledge or skills (professional or otherwise) enable organised crime groups to carry out their criminal activities, are another kind of interface. These facilitators can vary from public officials, to professionals and other facilitators, e.g. transport companies, landlords, hotel owners, taxi drivers and bouncers. To prevent the abuse of these facilitators, the national reports suggest an increase in the awareness of such abuse and the defensibility of the facilitators. Codes of conduct and the screening of personnel are important elements preventing the misuse of their services and their knowledge. Moreover, legislation such as the exclusion of criminals from public tender is a tool which shields against criminal involvement in public administration. In the case of legal professionals, organisations can invoke disciplinary law, which allows them to take disciplinary action without the interference of government.

Thirdly, criminal groups make use of other opportunities or tools present in the licit environment. These tools include the infrastructure of the licit environment, such as transport facilities and financial services. In the prevention of organised crime, the aim should be to diminish the availability of these tools for criminal purposes. For example, authorities can prohibit the establishment of legal persons when indications of a criminal past or affiliation exist. Anti-money laundering measures can be taken, however, governments should realise that they could lead to a displacement, that is, that alternative financial services and countries would be used, so safeguards also need to be taken to prevent this from happening.

In addition to these three categories of interfaces between the legitimate and illegitimate environment, the findings of the national reports gave rise to a close study of four important topics in this final report: the role of public administration and local businesses, legal professions, official and informal financial services, and forged official documents. With regard to each topic we discuss the facilitating opportunities, the measures that already have been taken and the possibilities of preventive action.

The role of public administration and local businesses

In order to conduct activities such as money laundering and the transport of illegal goods, criminal organisations depend on local government for obtaining permits and granting projects, and on the cooperation of local businesses. The key problem is the intermingling of legitimate and illicit worlds. These interfaces exist in the involvement of local businesses, which is a common phenomenon, and in corruption, which problem varies for each country. Preventing organised crime can therefore only be successful when businesses and governments possess a sufficient level of integrity. Existing measures therefore concern the integrity of public administration and local businesses, and the protection from abuse by external contacts.

The examples of best practice illustrate the importance of sharing relevant and reliable information, improving cooperation and increasing the responsibilities of all the parties concerned. With regard to the involvement of public administration, the 'administrative approach' in Amsterdam is a good example.

As a result of this approach, action is being taken on three fronts: in the integrity of the civil service apparatus, the screening of security processes concerning public tender procedures, and the infiltration of organised crime in certain areas and branches of industry in the city. The programme is a perfect example of an integrated and multi-agency approach in which the awareness of the risks of criminality are institutionalised in the entire bureaucratic and political organisation of Amsterdam. Furthermore, several agencies cooperate by sharing information and integral enforcement. With regard to business, the World Customs Organization provides successful cooperation between government and private entities on an international level. Such cooperation also takes place on local level. For example, in Rotterdam's main port, a risk assessment tool was set up by the authorities in association with various parties in the sea port's logistic chain. Moreover, in several countries the authorities have devised ways to supervise legal entities for fraud prevention purposes. To a large extent, these measures have not been especially established to prevent organised crime, but they are considered to be possible tools for that purpose. However, in some cases special regulations have been developed. In the Netherlands, the 'Vennoot' database system was set up to bring together relevant data on legal entities for crime prevention purposes.

Legal professions

The combination of financial and legal knowledge, and their aura of respectability and reliability, make lawyers attractive potential facilitators for organised crime. The involvement of a lawyer in a transaction can also create the impression of legitimacy. Moreover, the confidential nature of the lawyer/client relationship and the privilege of non-disclosure can be advantageous. It is important to emphasise that only limited empirical evidence exists on the involvement of lawyers in organised crime. In particular, the number of lawyers who actually perform acts for which they could be criminally prosecuted is very small. However, case studies show a number of lawyers rendering sophisticated forms of assistance by providing legal advice, credibility and facilities, which demonstrates the limitations of the notion that a lawyer is a person who merely defends their clients' cases in court.

Anti-money laundering laws are an important tool for preventing the involvement of lawyers. To a certain extent, the activities of lawyers have recently come under the scope of this legislation and they are therefore required to meet the disclosure obligation. These measures have far-reaching implications for certain specific professional rights, such as lawyer/client confidentiality and the privilege of non-disclosure, and they have been strongly opposed by members of the legal profession. However, the terrorist attack in the USA on 11 September 2001 fundamentally changed the situation and stifled the opposition of professional groups. The question is, however, what will be the effect of this new obligation to report unusual or suspect transactions. Up until now, the way in which law enforcement agencies have used information on suspicious financial transactions has not been particularly promising as only a tiny percentage of reports of suspicious transactions have actually lead to an investigation, at least, this is the case in the Netherlands.

With regard to best practice, both law enforcement and self-regulation should be increased. In anti-money laundering laws, observing confidentiality should be greater in genuine criminal defence cases and less where the information being protected relates to a business transaction. However, it is questionable whether such a theoretical distinction in activities would be applicable in the daily practice of the legal profession. Lawyers are inclined to argue that a thin line can be drawn between a business consultation on the one hand and legal advice on the other, as it is quite possible that their business consultation may eventually lead to a civil law suit and a court appearance. More research is necessary to find out whether such a distinction would be tenable.

With regard to self-regulation, it is evident that it is both possible and desirable to draw up professional rules according to which lawyers are prevented from behaving in compromising ways in relation to organised crime. Disciplinary boards may investigate lawyers and impose disciplinary measures on those who violate the rules of integrity. However, due to these boards' lack of investigative facilities and their limited accessibility for outsiders – such as law enforcement agencies and prosecutors – the 'self-cleansing' capacity of professional organisations has transpired to be very limited. The limited strength of disciplinary boards has demonstrated that, up until now, self-regulation alone is inadequate. In this, the central issue is the 'know your customer' principle. Lawyers must consider who the client is, what the client wants, whether the request is unusual and why they have been chosen to perform these particular services. It may also be worthwhile implementing a system of 'trusted representatives', that is, the use of consultants who could provide professional advice.

Official and informal financial services

There are several methods of transferring money. It can be transferred physically across borders and official banks can be used. Though both methods are appropriated for criminal purposes, the first is neither safe nor fast and the second has become less safe due to anti-money laundering legislation. Criminal organisations therefore tend to use money transfers. A money or value transfer service is a financial service which enables customers to deposit cash, cheques or other valuable goods at one location and which pays a corresponding sum in cash or another form of remuneration to someone at another location. The initial operator charges the customer a fee or percentage of the transfer amount. Money transfers are fast and easy, and their only disadvantage seems to be the high costs involved. This service is offered by two alternative remittance systems: legitimate non-banking financial institutes and informal money or transfer systems ('underground banking'). These services have been allocated 'red flags' in the national reports. The question is whether registration systems and security standards for money transfer services should be implemented or not. Regarding legitimate non-banking financial institutes, MoneyGram and Western Union Money Transfer are the only examples which currently offer licit money transfer systems worldwide. It is likely that some criminals have assumed that money transfers do not leave a trail and are not reported to investigative and financial intelligence units. Although MoneyGram's Internet document would certainly seem to support this, money transfer agencies are covered by anti-money laundering measures. The case studies indicate a weak spot in the fight against money laundering: monitoring and reporting are entrusted (under the threat of sanctions) to financial institutions who obviously have a commercial interest in not reporting suspicious transactions. It must be pointed out that the effectiveness of legislation not only depends on its presence, but also on the existence of a positive attitude in complying with the rules and the possibilities of enforcement: this is the difference between 'law in theory' and 'law in practice'. The central issue of the informal money or value transfer (IMVT) systems is that money is transferred outside the conventional banking system which is supervised and monitored by the competent authorities. The most critical element in this informal system is the presence of trust. Without mutual trust existing between operators and clients, IMVT systems cannot operate. They are considered to be attractive for transferring the proceeds of crime as individual money transfers through IMVT systems do not leave paper trails, in theory at least. However, in the Netherlands it transpired that the absence of a paper trail is a well-preserved myth. Many IMVT operators do require their customers to provide identification and this information is even faxed to one another. Moreover operators not only settle their accounts by adding up individual money transfers, but they also make use of the conventional banking system. With regard to best practice, the question is whether IMVT systems should be dealt with in exactly the same way as other remittance systems. Basically, strengthening supervision and control could have two divergent effects. On the one hand, it could provoke non-banking systems – in particular IMVT agencies – to go further underground. On the other hand, it might result in a situation in which the use of IMVT will no longer be advantageous in comparison with money transfers. Moreover, improving the infrastructure of basic financial services may lead to the situation in which the current legitimate users of IMVT will opt for money transfer systems instead.

In principle, two strategies can therefore be applied to money transfers. The first strategy simply involves a partial or full prohibition of money transfers by non-banking institutions. The second strategy concerns licensing the use of money transfers. A choice has to be made between prohibition or regulation and the latter option seems to be preferable. The FATF has recently developed a 'special recommendation VI' that brings all money or value transfer agencies (including 'underground bankers') within the ambit of the anti-money laundering regulations which already exist for the banking sector. However, opting for regulation has its drawbacks. A regulatory system which is not backed up by adequate administrative control might lead to serious problems.

Forged official documents

Forged Bills of Loading enable drugs to be safely concealed in containers and forged identity documents enable illegal immigrants to enter and reside in Western Europe. The case studies demonstrate that false identity documents are frequently used and contact amongst criminal groups in the area of stolen and counterfeited documents is prevalent. Although it is impossible to estimate the number of false documents in circulation, the problem is serious and society's interest in carrying out proper identity checks is increasing.

During the last few decades, the vulnerability of passports to fraud has decreased immensely. However, technical improvements have also resulted in improved forgeries: even hallmarked paper or extra layers of laminate can be imitated. To prevent the use of forgeries, European countries have established a computer database entitled the Edison Document System. This database contains the hallmarks of over 1,500 travel documents from all over the world. In addition to these technological improvements, governments have also established other measures. For example, in recent years more attention has been paid to the safe storage of blank passports. Furthermore, several countries now link their databases so that governments are able to prevent people from obtaining official identity documents under the name of a deceased person, for example. Checking social security numbers can also reveal identity fraud.

With respect to best practices, the possibilities for prevention basically consist of extending the existing measures, namely the continuing development of the technical enhancement of identity documents. Almost two hundred countries throughout the world distribute over ten thousand different identity papers, such as visas, birth certificates and driver's licenses. This demonstrates how much the global community would benefit from national and international standardisation. Even though global standardisation is not feasible, a continuation of European standardisation is certainly achievable. However, the detection of false documents does not solely depend on the above mentioned technical instruments. Ultimately, the most crucial element in successful and effective prevention is the commitment of the people who are in charge of checking documents. Despite the fact that we have open borders, border checks are still an important instrument. Inhabitants from over a hundred and thirty countries are required to be in possession of a so-called 'Schengen visa' if they wish to be admitted to a country within the Schengen zone. The better inspectors do their work, the more forged documents will be identified. This entails the checking of documents by airline companies who are legally obliged to adequately inspect their passengers' identity documents in pre-flight checks.

Conclusion

In order to prevent organised crime from abusing opportunities facilitated by the licit environment, it is of vital importance that governments, businesses and legal professions properly conduct their tasks of supervision and carry out checks. They basically function as the gatekeepers of the licit world and therefore all they have to be is aware, well-informed and unafraid to make choices.

A small increase in awareness could reduce the facilitating factor considerably. For example, with regard to immigrants who receive welfare service flats, a sheer unawareness often exists of the rules which stipulate the conditions under which a third party can or cannot be accommodated. Awareness should, however, involve more than just being knowledgeable about something. It is therefore of great importance to adopt legislation and concrete facilities which help people who dare to take action, e.g. drivers who refuse to transport suspicious cargo should be protected from customers' claims. Furthermore, awareness is not something that can be taken for granted. The parties involved have to recognise the importance of being aware. This applies to airline companies who have to conduct pre-boarding flight checks, as well as tax authorities who have to take into account the fact that criminals may try to inflate their turnover and profits as much as possible in order to legitimise proceeds of crime. Awareness presupposes good governance and at the very least, the integrity of its agencies, otherwise the situational approach would be totally ineffective.

Prevention is a matter of thinking and acting in advance and it is therefore necessary that decision makers are well informed. It is important to systematically gather information on the phenomenon of organised crime itself. As this study demonstrates, case studies could reveal information regarding the abuse of facilitators or the availability of logistic facilities. Such a form of 'knowledge-based prevention' is therefore recommended. However, some problems in the exchange of information between the participants will be encountered in an integral and preventive approach towards crime. Each agency has its own means of collecting information. This affects cooperation, particularly between services with completely different backgrounds, e.g. judicial and administrative agencies. It would be desirable to set up an agency which has legal status and the authorisation to check applications for permits, tender proposals etc. on the basis of all types of databases, and with the authorisation to force companies to cooperate with the agency's investigations.

Finally, it is important to recognise that the existence of organised crime may be beneficial for some institutions who are therefore not interested in the fight against it. For example, a balance would have to be achieved between checking harbour imports and exports, and the economic interests of the rapid circulation of goods. The importance of economic interests would be reduced if the European Union would standardise checks and supervision. Another important aspect is the principle of confidentiality of certain professions. In short, if governments attach a great importance to the prevention of organised crime, this has to be reflected in them making clear and distinct choices.

1 Introduction

Henk van de Bunt and Cathelijne van der Schoot[1]

This final report is part of the Falcone study entitled 'The Identification and Prevention of Opportunities that Facilitate Organised Crime'. The study aims to analyse criminal investigation files in order to identify opportunities for facilitating organised crime. The results may be used for the development of preventive strategies in the fight against organised crime.

The four participating countries, namely Finland, Hungary, Italy and the Netherlands, have each drawn up a report in which 15 cases of organised crime are described and analysed. The reports include 'red flags' – indications for possible preventive interventions – and present preventive measures. This final report comprises 'red flags' from the four national reports (Chapter 2) and the possibilities for the prevention of organised crime are outlined with regard to four topics. Chapter 3 elaborates upon the possibilities available to public administrations and local businesses to prevent unintentional interaction with organised crime groups. Chapter 4 discusses the preventive measures regarding the interaction between organised crime groups and the legal professions (lawyers). Chapters 5 and 6 describe measures regarding two important tools of organised crime, respectively: the abuse of official and informal financial services and forged official documents. Finally, a number of conclusions and recommendations in relation to the prevention of organised crime can be found in Chapter 7.

1.1 Organised crime prevention

1.1.1 What is the prevention of organised crime?

The concept of 'prevention' as well as that of 'organised crime' are rather vague. The combined use of both concepts can result in even more ambiguity. For example, divergent measures such as imposing the death penalty on perpetrators of organised crime as well as reporting suspicious transactions by banks to financial intelligence units, could both be categorised as the 'prevention of organised crime'. It is important to clarify what falls within the framework of the organised crime prevention and the scope of this project. In this study the 'organised crime prevention' concerns all the measures (laws and regulations) which have been established for fighting organised crime, except for measures pertaining to criminal law. The death penalty does not therefore fall under the definition, but all administrative measures and all measures undertaken by financial institutes do. Moreover, it is important how organised crime prevention policy is interpreted and which preventive measures have actually been implemented.

---

1   Henk van de Bunt is Professor in Criminology at Erasmus University Rotterdam and the Vrije Universiteit Amsterdam, and Cathelijne van der Schoot is PhD candidate at the Department of Criminology at Erasmus University Rotterdam.

Within the framework of the European Community, preventive action against organised crime has been launched on many fronts. Firstly, several *individual* measures aimed at the prevention of certain organised crime activities have come into force: e.g. anti-money laundering measures to prevent the abuse of the financial system.[2] Other measures include controlling the disposal of hazardous waste, preventing the smuggling of works of art and acting to halt the production of synthetic drugs. Furthermore, directives regarding accepting tenders and the grounds which have been formulated for excluding certain bidders from the tendering process, can also be perceived to be instruments to prevent or limit the penetration of organised crime into the public sector.[3]

The first signs of the European Union's *structural* needs for the prevention of organised crime date back to 1996, when the Stockholm conference examined the prevention of crime connected with European economic integration and social exclusion. The Treaty of Amsterdam then included the importance of the prevention of crime (organised or not) in policies of the European Union for the creation of an area of freedom, security and justice.[4] The *Action Plan to Combat Organised Crime* adopted by the European Council on 28 April 1997 stated that: "prevention is no less important than repression in any integrated approach to organised crime, to the extent that it aims at reducing the circumstances in which organised crime can operate. The Union should have the instruments to confront organised crime at each step on the continuum from prevention to repression and prosecution".[5] Section II of this plan continues to sum up a number of recommendations to make the preventive approach more specific:

– developing an anti-corruption policy within the government apparatus;
– making it possible to exclude persons convicted of offences relating to organised crime from tendering procedures; the investigation is further recommended of whether and under what circumstances – in view of legislation on personal confidentiality – individuals can be excluded "who are currently under investigation or prosecution"; and in this regard the plan states that instruments should be developed to enable the exchange of information between Member States and the European Community, and between Member States "both in administrative cooperation and the setting up of black-lists";
– collecting and the mutual exchange of information by member states on legal entities and natural persons – pursuant to regulations for the protection of personal information "as a means to prevent the penetration of organized crime in the public and legitimate private sector";
– devoting financial resources from various funds "to prevent larger cities in the Union from becoming breeding grounds for organized crime. Such funds

---

2 Council Directive on the prevention of the use of the financial system for the purpose of money laundering of 10 June 1991, *OJ L 166*, 28/06/1991, pp. 77-83.
3 European Parliament and Council Directive 97/52/EC of 13 October 1997 amending Directives 92/50/EEC, 93/36/EEC and 93/37/EEC concerning the coordination of procedures for awarding public service contracts, public supply contracts and public works contracts, *OJ L 328*, 28/11/1997, pp. 1-59.
4 This aspect was once again emphasised in the European Council Summit of Tampere in 1999, Presidency conclusions Tampere European Council of 15-16 October 1999, points 41-42 of the conclusion.
5 Action Plan of 28 April 1997 to combat organised crime, *OJ C251*, 15/08/1997, Section 5f.

can help those most at risk of exclusion from the labour market and thus alleviate the circumstances that could contribute to the development of organized crime";

– developing closer cooperation between EU Member States and the European Commission on combating fraud where the financial interests of the European Community are concerned;
– establishing an action programme to invest in the training of individuals who fulfil a key role in formulating and implementing preventative policy measures in the area of organised crime;
– and finally, introducing measures for the improved protection of certain vulnerable groups against the influence of organised crime, for example via codes of conduct.[6]

The innovative aspect of this preventive approach is the fact that it is not primarily aimed at the perpetrators of organised crime, but rather at the various circumstances which facilitate organised crime. The preventive approach addresses governments, civilians and enterprises and it attempts to make them feel responsible for reducing the opportunities for organised crime.

Since 1997, the subject of organised crime prevention has always been on the agenda of the European Union which has encouraged all kinds of initiatives in this field. In line with this development, the Council urged the Commission to finalise the 1997 Action Plan in their Resolution of 21 December 1998 and provide additional elements on the EU strategy.[7]

In this policy of fostering knowledge on the prevention of organised crime and improving the exchange of information amongst Member States, the European Council has adopted exchange, training and cooperation programmes to combat organised crime, namely the so-called Falcone programme[8] and the Hippocrates programme.[9] In the meanwhile both programmes are enclosed in AGIS, a new programme on police and judicial cooperation in criminal matters.[10] After the publication of the Action Plan, the European council published a new plan in May 2000.[11] The general ideas of the Action Plan are reiterated in the new plan, but it also contained several new proposals in relation to the prevention of organised crime. They include proposals to improve sharing information between the

6 Action Plan of 28 April 1997 to combat organised crime, *OJ C251*, 15/08/1997, Section II.
7 Council Resolution of 21 December 1998 on the Prevention of Organized Crime with Reference to the Establishment of a Comprehensive Strategy for Combating it, *OJ C 408*, 29/12/98, pp. 1-4.
8 Joint Action of 19 March 1998 adopted by the Council, on the basis of Article K.3 of the Treaty on European Union, establishing a programme of exchanges, training and cooperation for persons responsible for action to combat organised crime (Falcone programme), *OJ L 099*, 31/03/1998, pp. 8-12.
9 Proposal for a Council Decision establishing a programme of incentives and exchanges, training and cooperation for the prevention of crime (Hippocrates programme), *OJ C 96 E*, 27/03/2001, pp. 244-246.
10 Programme for police and judicial cooperation in criminal matters (Programme AGIS) – Annual work programme and call for applications for 2003, *OJ C 5*. 10/01/03, pp. 5-18.
11 The prevention and control of organised crime: a European Union strategy for the beginning of the new millennium, *OJ C 124*, 03/05/2000.
12 The prevention and control of organised crime: a European Union strategy for the beginning of the new millennium, *OJ C 124*, 03/05/2000, pp. 1-33.

Members States and the European Commission, and to make information on
successful approaches and best practices available on a local and national level.[12]
In addition to a preventive policy against organised crime, the European Union
also stresses the importance of the penal repression of organised crime and the
effective cooperation between police and judicial services in different countries.
The Treaty of Amsterdam proclaimed the importance of closer police and judicial
cooperation to provide citizens "with a high level of safety within an area of
freedom, security and justice".[13] The Action Plan of 1997 contains the
recommendation that judicial cooperation should be increased to the same level
as police cooperation and that Europol's mandate should be expanded.[14] In
addition, there are developments in relation to the joint investigation teams and
Eurojust. Such developments may even mean that the repressive approach
assumes a more prominent place than the preventive one.
Finally, the fight against organised crime has taken on new urgency since the
terrorist attacks in 2001. According to the FATF, the fight against organised crime
and terrorism go hand in hand. In a recent report they stated that criminal
organisations and terrorist groups basically use the same methods in hiding and
obscuring the links between the source, destination or purposes of their finances
(FATF, 2003: 3). Although it is questionable whether organised crime and
terrorism should be connected, the focus on terrorism has up until now
accelerated the implementation of certain measures against organised crime,
both preventive as well as repressive ones.

1.1.2 Situational crime prevention

The situational crime prevention approach is central to this study. Its theoretical
assumption is that the level of crime – including organised crime – is determined
by the presence of facilitating situational factors, e.g. the presence of attractive
targets, a low level of supervision and low risk of apprehension. Criminal activities
therefore have to be analysed to reveal the facilitating role of situational factors.
Clarke refers to this as a "criminal script of tactical and logistical actions" which
consists of "series of actions and conditions necessary for the commission of the
offences".[15] Due to the logistic processes of organised crime, individual events
should systematically map out "the immediate causal preconditions which have
to be met for the event to occur". Intervention in these preconditions will reduce
the opportunities for the events to take place. Clarke named this the crime
prevention approach and he divided it into five different steps (Clarke, 1997):
1   Collection of data about the nature and dimensions of a specific crime
    phenomenon;

---

13 Treaty of Amsterdam amending the treaty on European Union, the treaties establishing the European
    Communities and related acts, *OJ C 340,* 10/11/1997, Title VI.
14 Action Plan of 28 April 1997 to combat organised crime, *OJ C251,* 15/08/1997, Chapter V.
15 Home Office Research Development and Statistics Directorate, NCIS, Swedish Crime Prevention Council,
    Europol (2001), *The Identification, Development and Exchange of Good Practice for Reducing Organised Crime*
    (draft version March 2001), p. 5.

2   Analysis of the situational conditions which permit or facilitate the
    commission of the crime under consideration;
3   Study of possible instruments aimed at blocking the opportunities for this
    kind of crime;
4   Implementation of the chosen measures;
5   Evaluation of the results and dissemination of the good practices.

Inspired by his ideas, we attribute significant importance to the case studies.
The four participating countries were requested to describe and analyse a
number of typical cases (drug trafficking, smuggling illegal immigrants and
women trafficking)[16] which could provide the basis for identifying facilitating
opportunities. The case studies did indeed reveal certain aspects or events which
facilitated organised crime activities. Particular attention was devoted to the
'contact points' between the licit and illicit environment. Even though criminal
networks try to conceal their activities, they always require the cooperation or
services of the licit environment.

If a façade is to be created in order to conduct criminal activities, a legal person
will have to be bought or created and the help of the licit environment is thus
required. In doing this, the help of other licit operators, e.g. transport companies,
financial institutes etc. will also be required. These necessary 'contact points'
between the licit and illicit environment form 'bridges' between these worlds,
creating opportunities for organised crime and these opportunities can be
regarded as 'red flags' by law enforcers.

1.2   Methodology

As mentioned in the title, the research is aimed at identifying and preventing
opportunities for organised crime. In order to achieve this two research questions
were formulated:
1   What kind of opportunities which facilitate organised crime can be
    distinguished?
2   What preventive measures could be taken in order to reduce these crime
    risks?

In order to answer these two main questions, the research was divided into two
phases. The first phase consists of national analyses of organised crime cases, in
order to detect the bridges between the illicit and licit environment which

---

16   The smuggling of illegal immigrants and women trafficking both involve the illegal crossing of borders. The
     major difference between these two activities is that, in the case of women trafficking, women are exploited
     for sexual or economic reasons and, in the case of smuggling illegal immigrants, people pay to cross the
     borders. A distinction can thus be drawn between victimisation and voluntariness. Illegal immigrants who are
     in some way exploited to pay for their journey nevertheless still belong to the first category.
17   Due to the confidentiality of data in police records and the risks of law suites it was decided not to publish
     the national reports.

present opportunities for preventive measures to take place. The results of these national analyses were described in four national reports. The reports are confidential so they have not been included in this report.[17] However, their essential conclusions are summarised in Chapter 2. The remaining chapters (which cover the second phase of the research) present some of the most important problems and certain starting points for preventing them. In each chapter the findings of the four national reports are referred to.

1.2.1 First phase: the national case analyses

Files of closed police investigations of criminal groups were an important source for this study. This direct access to police files or case studies is quite unique for empirical researchers. The advantages are that the researcher works with reliable and valid data, which is checked by the research team itself. We had a similar structure for the analyses of the files and the description of the case studies. Firstly, the participating countries were requested to describe and analyse 15 cases that fell under the following definition of organised crime: "groups primarily focused on illegal profits, who systematically commit crimes that adversely affect society and who are capable of effectively shielding their activities, in particular by being willing to use physical violence or corruption" (Fijnaut *et al.*, 1998: 27).

The researchers of the participating countries had difficulties working with the definition we provided. It was therefore decided that each country could use a definition of their own choice although the key elements of our definition were retained. This meant we were working with a definition of organised crime that was both wide-ranging (not restricted to mafia-type organisations or to organisations merely interested in their dominion of certain regions or branches) and at the same time discriminatory (excluding corporate crime, not restricted to incidental crimes). The various definitions used by the participants complied with

---

18   The Italian report uses the UN definition of organised crime. According to this definition an organised criminal group is "a structured group of three or more persons, existing for a period of time and acting in concert with the aim of committing one or more serious crimes or offences established in accordance with this Convention, in order to obtain, directly or indirectly, financial or other material benefits" (United Nations Convention Against Transnational Organised Crime, Palermo, Italy, December 2000, art. 3). The Finish report refers to the definition of organised crime as used in the context of the Annual European Union Organised Crime Situation Report. In this, in order to speak about organised crime it must have at least six of the following characteristics, four of which must be those numbered 1, 3, 5 and 11: (1) Collaboration of more than 2 people; (2) Each person has their own appointed tasks; (3) Operating for a prolonged or indefinite period of time (refers to the stability and - potential - durability); (4) Some form of discipline and control is being used; (5) Under suspicion of committing serious criminal offences; (6) Operating at an international level; (7) Violence or another means suitable for intimidation is being used; (8) Commercial or businesslike structures are being used; (9) It is engaged in money laundering; (10) It is exerting influence on politics, the media, public administration, judicial authorities or the economy; (11) It is determined by the pursuit of profit and/or power (K4 Committee, Elaboration of a common mechanism for the collection and systematic analysis of information on international organised crime, Enfopol 161, rev. I, The Council of the European Union, Brussels, 1994). The Hungarians used the description in their Criminal Code, § 137 (Section 4) of which states: "conspiracy which is based on the distribution of the responsibilities, a hierarchical system, and roles which are built on personal relations. The conspiracy is established to make profit by committing crimes.".

19   However, a few cases were too old and some of them lacked a court decision.

these basic conditions and could therefore be accepted as working definitions.[18] In 2000 it was then decided that only cases which had been decided upon in court – at least in the first instance of the proceedings – in the last three years (1997-2000) could be selected. This criterion was developed in order to avoid the use of old cases although the cases had to accumulate a sufficient amount of evidence to bring them to court. On the whole, the four countries complied with this request.[19] A third criterion for the selection concerned the subject of the cases. Initially it had been decided to limit the selection of the cases to three forms of organised crime: women trafficking, the smuggling of illegal immigrants and drug trafficking. Based on the difficulties the Italian researchers had in distinguishing between the first two categories, it was decided that these categories could be combined as different forms of illegal migration. According to the guidelines, the selection was also based on interviews with key public officials, namely public prosecutors, law enforcement officials or other experts in the fight against women trafficking, the smuggling of illegal immigrants and drug trafficking.

This selection resulted in 15 cases for each country. The Netherlands had several cases on the three issues: 4 cases on women trafficking, 4 cases on the smuggling of illegal immigrants and 7 cases on drug trafficking. Italy selected 3 cases on the trafficking in drugs and 12 cases on the smuggling of illegal immigrants and women trafficking. Finland and Hungary limited their cases to one type of organised crime. The Finish report focused solely on the drug trade. During the selection it appeared that the cases on women trafficking and the smuggling of illegal immigrants did not meet the criteria of organised crime. The Hungarian cases all concern smuggling illegal immigrants. The reporters could not find any detailed cases of woman trafficking and drug trafficking because these two types of crime are considered by the police to be "transit crime": crimes which only pass through the country. In this context, Hungary can be considered to be a transit country and not a target country. Because the Hungarian authorities usually hand on the information to the officials in the target countries, there are only a limited number of records of cases in Hungary. Due to new legislation concerning women trafficking which came into force in 1999, some cases of women trafficking in Hungary do exist. However, gathering evidence concerning such cases proved to be so difficult that when the Hungarian national report was drawn up, no cases had yet been brought to court.

The most important method of standardising the research activities of the four countries was by using a checklist. To overcome any possible lack of clarity, an extensive checklist with instructions, clarifications and examples regarding the questions was drawn up.[20] The checklist elaborates upon the following leading questions:

1   How is the criminal group structured and what are the main illegal activities?

---

19   However, a few cases were too old and some of them lacked a court decision.
20   The extended version of the questionnaire can be found in Appendix 1.

2   What is the composition of the criminal group and how do they operate (what is their *modus operandi*)?
3   How do the criminal groups interact with the illicit environment?
4   How do the criminal groups interact with the licit environment?

This checklist enabled the researchers to gain insight into the facilitating opportunities of organised crime and to pinpoint any possibilities for interventions to prevent these facilitating opportunities from being misused. So, the methodology produces a knowledge-based form of prevention.

Finally, it should be emphasised that the national reports were written in 2001 and 2002. This means that the characteristics of organised crime and the fight against it as presented in the national reports are not always up to date. In particular, the situation in Hungary is changing under the influence of international political and economic processes. Due to Hungary joining the European Union, the country has adopted new regulations. Moreover, the recent hostile situations in Afghanistan and Iraq could also have had an influence on the situation in Hungary.

1.2.2 Second phase: the in-depth studies

Various in-depth studies were conducted regarding four major 'bridges' between the illicit and licit environment based on the outcome of the red flags in the four national reports. The goal of these in-depth studies was to detect any possible preventive measures. Four relevant themes were discerned which form the topics of discussion in four chapters in this report:
1   The role of public administration and local business;
2   The role of legal professions;
3   Transferring proceeds of crime;
4   The forgery of identity documents.

In each chapter we discuss the question of whether or not there is a problem and/or whether organised crime is involved. For instance, is there any proof or knowledge that public administrations and organised crime have become intertwined; is there any evidence of organised crime penetrating the public administration? Subsequently, we describe the measures that have already been taken to tackle the problem, we then discuss the best practices which are already available and what preventive measures could possibly still be taken. Each chapter concludes with a reference to the possibilities of preventive action.

2 'Red flags' and the measures presented in the national reports

Cathelijne van der Schoot[21]

The most important issue in this study is the identification of contacts between organised crime groups and the licit environment. These contacts are of vital importance to the existence and subsistence of organised crime. In the context of organised crime prevention, it is important that the number of instances of these contacts is reduced. Based on the national analyses of police investigations, some opportunities which facilitate organised crime have been revealed and these opportunities have been allocated so-called 'red flags'. These red flags thus address the moments and possibilities where preventive measures can be taken. This chapter will provide a survey of the red flags[22] and the proposed measures[23] in the four national reports concerning the three subjects of the study: women trafficking, the smuggling of illegal immigrants and drug trafficking. For detailed descriptions of the red flags please see the national reports.[24]

From an analysis of all the red flags it is evident that contact between the illicit and licit environment falls into three categories: the demand for illegal products and services from the licit environment, the abuse of facilitators in the licit environment and the availability of "tools" in the licit environment. Firstly, the demand from the licit environment for illegal products and services forms a breeding ground for organised crime groups. A category of preventive measures is therefore aimed at reducing this demand. Secondly, contact between the illicit and licit environments concern 'facilitators', people whose knowledge or services can be abused by criminals for criminal purposes. These facilitators can vary from lawyers who are able to set up illegal financial constructions to harbour employees who have access to information on boarding times and landing places. To prevent the abuse of these facilitators, the national reports suggest an increase in the awareness of such abuse and the defensibility of the facilitators. Thirdly, criminal groups make use of opportunities or tools present in the licit environment for their criminal activities. These tools include the infrastructure of the licit environment, such as transport facilities and financial services. In the prevention of organised crime, the aim should be to diminish the availability of these tools for criminal purposes.

As described in the national reports, the effectiveness of preventive measures depends on a number of conditions.[25] In this survey, in addition to preventive

---

21 Cathelijne van der Schoot is PhD candidate at the Department of Criminology at Erasmus University Rotterdam.
22 For a summary of the opportunities which facilitate crime detected in the national reports see appendix 2.
23 For a summary of the preventive measures presented in the national reports see appendix 3.
24 In this survey it is important to realise that the facilitating opportunities from the Dutch and Italian reports are based on all three issues: drug trafficking, the smuggling of illegal immigrants and women trafficking. However, the red flags from the Hungarian and Finnish report are only based on cases of, respectively, human smuggling and cases of drug trafficking.
25 These conditions apply to the approach to organised crime as whole, including preventive as well as repressive measures.

measures three important preconditions will be described, i.e. the need for unambiguous legislation and regulation, efficient law enforcement and the exchange of information.

2.1   Reducing the demand for illegal products and services

The existence of a demand for products and services is the key to survival in the business world. Such a condition also applies to organised crime groups. Influencing the demand will in turn influence the trade in illegal products and services, so that the prevention of organised crime can be realised by attempting to diminish the demand for illegal services and goods.[26] It is evident that influencing the demand largely depends on the nature of the criminal activity, for example, the illegal trade in chemical waste is connected with the behaviour of legal enterprises; tackling the illegal drug trade is related to the decrease in the number of drug users. A reduction in the trafficking of women relates to the reduction in the demand by brothels for illegal foreign prostitutes. In cases relating to the smuggling of illegal immigrants, there should be a reduction in the demand of people wanting to leave their country of origin to build up a better life elsewhere, to be reunited with their family or to earn enough money abroad to support their family in the country of origin.

These examples display the global and general character of the measures. After all, what is more effective than improving people's social conditions to prevent them from being tempted into becoming involved in human smuggling, women trafficking and drug abuse? What else could be done other than improving living conditions or implementing structural measures in the labour market?

It is possible to influence demand through legislation. Though politically unrealistic, the legalisation of drugs would stop the demand for illegal products. Consumers could purchase their products legally. In 2002, the Netherlands legalised the exploitation of prostitution, lifting the prohibition on brothels. The checks on brothels exercised under the scope of the regulation enable the authorities to detect women who are working in brothels against their will, or who are working without a working or residence permit. This is intended to decrease the demand of brothel owners for victims of women trafficking.[27]

Another example of prevention through legislation is the 'Benefit Entitlement (Residence Status) Act' (*Koppelingswet*) which links persons' use of government facilities to their residence permit.[28] This means that illegal immigrants

---

26 Besides influencing the demand, one can also attempt to influence the supply, e.g. potential victims in the countries of origin should be provided with information about the possibilities and limitations of legal migration and the risks of exploitation linked to women trafficking and illegal immigration. This would make recruitment more difficult.

27 Although the first effects of this new law have been evaluated (Daalder, 2002), it is not yet possible to say what the precise effects are on the involvement of organised crime groups.

28 This Act amends the Alien Act and several other laws concerning the rights of aliens towards administrative bodies regarding provisions, facilities, benefits, exemptions and permits relating to the legal residence of foreigners in the Netherlands (*Koppelingswet*), Act of 26 March 1998, the Netherlands Statute book (*Stbl.*) 1998, 203.

are excluded from government facilities and legal claims for permits and exemptions.[29] This law aims to prevent the continuance of illegal residence and the false appearance of legitimacy. In addition, the law dissuades employers from contacting illegal workers, which decreases the demand for illegal labour. Since illegal immigrants usually perform illegal labour, this law also influences the demand for human trafficking. However, these restrictive measures could cause a displacement effect as illegal labourers may shift their activities deeper into the criminal circuit.

2.2 Increase the defensibility of facilitators in the licit environment

Organised crime groups try to establish contact with facilitators in the licit environment for criminal purposes. According to the four national reports, the following facilitators are the most common: public officials, legal professionals, transport companies, lodging-house companies, landlords, hotel owners and taxi drivers. These facilitators possess particular knowledge or skills (professional or otherwise) which enable organised crime groups to carry out their criminal activities. In such cases we can speak of facilitators being subject to abuse. A large amount of the contact between criminals and facilitators is unavoidable, as officials or legal professionals are unaware that their services are being used for criminal purposes. Nevertheless, case studies in the national reports suggest that in some situations service providers should have been suspicious, but due to ignorance or negligence they could not or would not acknowledge the signals. This means that preventive measures should be aimed at increasing awareness and integrity. Tools would then be required to improve the defensibility of the facilitators.

Public officials
The national reports frequently indicate corruption or dishonourable behaviour, e.g. police officers who leak information or bribed surveillance officers. Even though this mostly occurs in Eastern Europe, there is also evidence of it existing in Western countries.
All the national reports stress the necessity of a strong degree of integrity in all areas of government. An important element in the fight against corruption consists of both repressive as well as preventive measures. Preventive measures consist of codes of conduct and the screening of personnel. Situational and organisational measures, such as increasing hierarchical or collegial supervision, can also lead to a decrease in corruption.
However, increased integrity alone will not suffice. Tools need to be provided which allow active shielding against criminal involvement to take place. One of the most important measures in this area is the exclusion from public tender. This preventive measure originates from the first principle of the European Union.

29 Exceptions for exclusion concern education, legal support and medical care in emergency situations.

It provides the tendering government a legal basis to assess the integrity and criminal involvement of companies which apply for a tender contract. Italy and the Netherlands have implemented legislation to allow the tendering government to refuse permits or to exclude legal persons from rendering procedures in cases where they are suspected of criminal activities (see Chapter 3).

Professionals
In order to conduct their criminal activities, criminal organisations also subject the legal professions to abuse. According to the national reports, this abuse mostly concerns legal professions such as lawyers, legal advisors, notaries, auditors, accountants and tax consultants. These legal professions facilitate organised crime groups by providing judicial and financial expertise. It is difficult to eliminate the contact between the legal professions and criminals; in many cases professionals are not aware that their services are being used for criminal purposes. Despite this, however, there are cases of culpable involvement. According to Fijnaut *et al.* (1998: 126) culpable involvement can be divided into two categories: actual culpable involvement and negligence. Culpable involvement means that the professionals are aware of the illegality of their client's activities. Negligence refers to situations in which the culpable involvement of professionals cannot be ascertained, but where warning signals were present, the professionals should have been alerted. Just like negligent public officers, these professionals could and should have known they were facilitating criminal activities.

In cases of culpable involvement it is possible to establish preventive counter-measures. As with the public officials, the first category of measures concerns the increase of the integrity and the awareness of these professionals. Professional organisations, to which these professionals belong, have taken special measures. Firstly, codes of conduct have been created and the behaviour of individual professionals is being monitored. Secondly, organisations can invoke disciplinary law, which allows them to take disciplinary action against professionals, without the interference of government (see Chapter 4).

Moreover, European legislation has provided legal professions with a tool for increasing their defensibility. The extension of the disclosure obligation for financial institutions to – amongst others – the legal professions has provided the latter with a limited obligation to report cases of suspicious criminal behaviour. This allows them to refuse certain services and report suspicions without violating their professional obligation of secrecy (see Chapter 4).

Other facilitators
Criminal organisations make use of all kinds of other facilitators: transport companies, lodging-house companies, landlords, hotel owners, taxi drivers, bouncers, bailiffs and car rental services. In these cases, the first measures should also be aimed at increasing awareness and integrity. Facilitators should screen their customers and refuse to participate in criminal activities. Since these cases concern commercial enterprises, it is inevitable that problems of a commercial

nature will arise. Governments therefore have to convince these enterprises that cooperation with criminals can jeopardize their companies and lead to unfair competition within the sector. In order to prevent such involvement with criminals, sector organisations have analysed their own vulnerabilities and designed a so-called toolkit to deal with them. Additionally, sectors have created codes of conduct and governments have implemented regulations to protect the position of informers (Chapter 3).

Furthermore, the government has given commercial facilitators tools. The disclosure obligation in the European measures against money laundering has been extended to traders in valuable goods. This extension requires particular companies to report certain payments and suspicions of criminal activities to a financial intelligence unit. However, due to commercial interests, only a restricted form of government intervention is permitted.

2.3   Reducing the availability of tools in the licit environment

In contrast to measures which are aimed to influence the behaviour of the buyers of illegal products and services, namely the behaviour of public officials and others who too easily make their services and knowledge available to criminals, the third category refers to situational crime prevention. Such preventive measures consist of restricting the possibilities for using or owning tools which may facilitate criminal activities.

In theory, many tools exist which may be used for criminal activities. For example, there are legal persons who feign legal trade, cars which transport illegal products and hotel lobbies which function as meeting places for criminals, etc.. The national reports suggest a number of tools that are frequently used by criminal groups, the availability of which can be decreased: for instance, forged documents, legal persons and financial services.

Forged documents
Organised crime groups make use of forged documents in various circumstances, e.g. to enable illegal immigrants, trafficked women or criminals who are wanted by the police to cross borders. To reduce the opportunity of forging documents or the availability of forged documents, the national reports have presented various measures. Firstly, governments should pay more attention to the security of places where official documents are stored, e.g. town halls, to counteract the theft of blank passports. Greater security measures should also apply to the materials which are used to fabricate official documents, such as copper stamps and watermarks. Secondly, official documents should be made foolproof, making forgery almost impossible or at the very least, more difficult. To this end, modern techniques such as biometrics could be used. Finally, greater investments should be made in the verification of documents. Customs should have well-educated employees and hi-tech equipment at their disposal (Chapter 6).

Legal persons
Organised crime groups subject legal persons to abuse to shield their illegal activities. It is obviously not possible to completely prevent the use of legal persons by criminals. If no indications of a criminal past or affiliation exist, the competent authorities may not prohibit the establishment of a legal person. Nevertheless, measures to tackle the abuse of legal persons are available. More detailed information on this topic can be found in other critical studies.[30]

Traditional and non-traditional financial institutes
By opening banking accounts, changing money, transferring money through financial institutes, etc. organised crime groups are able to launder their illegal profits and invest in the licit environment. Together with measures against the abuse of financial services, measures against the abuse of public procurement are the first preventive measures against organised crime. The European Union provides a Directive on the prevention of money laundering which contains several obligations. The obligation to identify customers prevents criminals from undertaking anonymous action. The obligation to report suspicious transactions increases the risks involved in carrying out money transfers by non-banking financial institutions. As a result of these measures, organised crime groups are moving their activities to other countries. One of the preventive measures thus aims at instructing these countries and strengthening their defences. These measures may cause a displacement effect on informal banking systems, such as underground banking. Possible preventive measures against non-banking financial institutions and informal financial services are described in Chapter 5.

2.4 Conditional measures

The effectiveness of preventive measures depends on a number of conditions. The four national reports note the following as being the most important: the need for unambiguous legislation and regulation, efficient law enforcement and the exchange of information.

Unambiguous legislation and regulation
In order to fight illegal activities a basis in criminal law is obviously required, i.e. such activities should be described as offences. The national reports demonstrate that even for such an activity as women trafficking, this is not always the case. In the Italian criminal code there is no specific offence entitled 'trafficking in human beings'. Certain other overlapping offences can be used, however, the lack of simplicity may be an obstacle in fighting women trafficking. Moreover, some

---

30 See for example Transcrime, *Euroshore; Protecting the EU financial system from the exploitation of financial centres and offshore facilities by organised crime*, Trento: University of Trento, 2000 and Transcrime, *Transparency and Money Laundering*, Trento: University of Trento, 2001. Both studies analyse company law (in a wide range of countries), which provides opportunities for exploitation by criminals.

offences are punishable under law, but the legal definition is ambiguous and inadequate, which means it can be abused by criminal groups. Dutch legislation regarding the smuggling of human beings is an example of such ambiguous legislation; a 'hole' in the legislation penalises the entrance of illegal immigrants into the Netherlands, while their departure from the Netherlands to a non-Schengen country is not punishable.[31]

The lack of legislation or ambiguous legislation can hinder the fight on both a national and international level. It is therefore necessary to screen legislation for 'holes' which facilitate criminal activities. Furthermore, discrepancies between the countries also facilitate criminal activities. It is therefore necessary to take further steps to harmonise criminal laws in both the European Union and elsewhere. This is also likely to apply to unifying sanctions, so that organised crime groups do not displace their activities to more vulnerable countries.

Efficient law enforcement

The enormous illegal profits made by organised crime and the extensive influence organised crime exerts on society illustrate the importance of a repressive fight against it. However, the fight against organised crime does have its limitations and policy makers diverge in their approach to different criminal activities. Different countries thus concentrate on different activities. Moreover, for example, although Hungary included anti-money laundering legislation in the Criminal Code in 1994, the lack of financial and human resources for such thorough investigations has prevented any money laundering cases from being taken to court. In addition to political interest, efficient law enforcement requires well-equipped law enforcement services: this means that a sufficient number of well-educated personnel and modern equipment should be available. This does not only apply to police investigation teams, but also to Customs authorities and public administration. The importance of a joint approach towards organised crime should lead to an expansion of the common policy on justice and home affairs, and simultaneously increase investments in such a policy.

Exchange of information

The main difference between the repressive and preventive fight against organised crime lies in those who execute the policy. Repressive policies are executed by investigative police services, whereas preventive policy is executed by other services, e.g. public administration and financial institutes.

The involvement of non-police services in the fight against organised crime would entail the establishment of a new form of cooperation and information exchange. Cooperation and the exchange of information should take place not only on a national and international level but also throughout all aspects of society. Anti-money laundering has after all led to a situation in which financial

---

31 The minister of Justice recently submitted a legislative proposal for fighting the smuggling of illegal immigrants. This bill provides for a wider penalisation of the smuggling of illegal immigrants, as the smuggling to all European Union countries will be made punishable (http://www.justitie.nl/pers/berichten/index.asp).

institutions and, as of recently, legal professions are required to report certain well-defined transactions, in order to facilitate criminal investigations. Moreover, other government agencies require police information in order to screen companies that are involved in public tendering.

The new need for the exchange of information has its limitations on a national and international level, especially with regard to privacy and data protection. However, further research into these new forms of information exchange has demonstrated that organised crime prevention is a valid legal reason for sharing data (Seger, 2003: 21).

2.5 The 4 selected topics for in-depth studies

The survey in the previous section demonstrates that preventive measures fall into three categories: a reduction in the demand for illegal products and services, an increase in the defensibility of facilitators in the licit environment and a reduction of the availability of tools in the licit environment. Several persons could be distinguished in the contacts between the illicit and licit environment. These concern public officers, legal professionals and other facilitators in the licit environment. We therefore reached the conclusion that these facilitators should be the subjects of in-depth studies. Furthermore, due to the significance attached to the forgery of documents in the national reports, this should also be subject to in-depth study.

The four selected subjects will be described in four different chapters: The role of public administration and local businesses (Chapter 3); Legal professions (Chapter 4); Official and informal financial services (Chapter 5); and Forged official documents (Chapter 6).

3 The role of public administration and local businesses

Wim Huisman and Peter Klerks[32]

In this chapter we will look at the role of the government and local business in the prevention of organised crime. To a certain extent, organised crime requires the services of the public administration and local business. In order to conduct the activities of money laundering, racketeering practices or creating a legal facade, criminal organisations depend on local government for obtaining permits, outsourcing work and granting projects. Furthermore, they need the cooperation of financial institutions to transfer money. This means that there is a risk of corruption; civil servants, employees or local politicians could be bribed in order to obtain the service in question. This risk exists alongside that of law enforcement officers being bribed for not taking action against criminal operations. With regard to logistics, criminal organisations require the help of legal commercial services. As a consequence, businesses could act as facilitators with or without their knowledge. There is also the risk that criminal organisations could set up their own businesses in order to facilitate their own activities. The threat of corruption and the abuse of public and commercial businesses for criminal purposes therefore pose a challenge, but also an opportunity for taking action.

Two types of measures could be taken. First, internal measures could be taken to prevent corruption within the governmental apparatus and business enterprises. Such an approach would be an attempt to guard the integrity of the representatives of public administration and the commercial sector. Second, external measures could be taken to prevent the use of public and commercial services for criminal purposes. Such an approach would aim at preventing the facilitation of organised crime. Before examining these two approaches further, we will first focus on the key problem of the involvement of governmental agencies and commercial institutions in organised crime.

3.1 The key problem: the intermingling of legitimate and illicit worlds

3.1.1 The corruption of public officers

A well-known ramification of organised crime is corruption. Criminal organisations bribe public officials, employees and law enforcement agents in order to obtain certain services or to persuade them not to take action against them. Corruption is one of the elements in the definition of organised crime which is used by the European Union.

Each year, Transparency International, the world's leading non-governmental organisation fighting corruption, ranks countries in a corruption perception

32   Wim Huisman is lecturer at the Department of Criminology at the Vrije Universiteit Amsterdam. Peter Klerks, who wrote sections 3.2 and 3.3, is Senior Researcher at the Research Unit of the Dutch Police Academy.

index. In 2002, the level of corruption in 102 countries was studied, including the four countries which participated in the Falcone project. Finland ranked first as the country with the lowest level of corruption. The Netherlands were number seven and Italy and Hungary ranked close to each other, respectively thirty-first and thirty-third. In accordance with its first-place position, the Finnish report does not include any case which involves corruption, despite the rise of criminal organisations from Estonia and Russia. This is not the case in the other studies. The Dutch report only mentions some indications of corruption. In one case, two police officers were leaking information about police actions against brothels and were offering advice on how to conduct woman trafficking and exploit brothels. The most significant case of corruption was a civil servant who predated entry stamps in the passports of trafficked women and gave them working permits. He also ensured that immigration officers did not visit the brothel during a certain period of time. Some of the other cases showed totally negligent law enforcers and civil servants. Although this did not involve corruption as such, the law enforcers should have known that the situation was not legitimate. The same applies to the aliens police who in several cases were far too lenient in distributing residence permits and stamping passports. Although it has not been proven that such action was corrupt, it is evident that the aliens police were too permissive and they behaved with great negligence. It is a remarkable fact that in the Netherlands there are only a few corruption cases concerning the trafficking of drugs. This can probably be explained by the large number of opportunities for carrying out these activities, such as the infrastructure of seaports in Rotterdam and Amsterdam and the limited efforts to check the borders which make bribery unnecessary.

A large degree of corruption was evident in the cases in the Italian report in which it was established in ten out of fifteen cases. In cases concerning the smuggling of illegal immigrants, the Italian study reports the corruption of public officials en route in order to obtain the necessary visas, to 'oil the palms' of custom officers and persuade border police officials 'to look the other way'.

In the Hungarian report, no signs of large-scale corruption were found. However, the Hungarian authorities have detected some cases of corruption. According to figures of the Hungarian Police's Directorate against Organised Crime, 17 criminal groups have contacts in and influence on public administration, 18 groups in criminal justice, 11 groups in political life and 35 groups in law enforcement organisations.

On the basis of these national reports, we can conclude that, with the exception of Finland, there is evidence of the corruption of governmental agents by perpetrators of organised crime.

3.1.2 Involvement of local businesses

In the Finish, Hungarian, Italian and Dutch case studies several examples of licit businesses owned by criminals or businesses which act as facilitators can be found. The Italian report mentions licit businesses which are owned by criminals and which are used to invest criminal money or to provide a cover for an illicit business. In relation to the smuggling of illegal immigrants and women trafficking, the reports state that in almost all the cases which were analysed, there were hotel owners, people renting flats and houses, and taxi drivers who indirectly aided and abetted criminal activities.

The Finnish report shows that several Estonian and Russian leaders of organised criminal groups were running substantial legal businesses in addition to carrying out criminal activities. Criminal leaders seem to be the most active in the transport, construction and the hotel and catering industry, but this does not exclude other branches. Several leading perpetrators were active in the information technology business. The Finnish study shows that criminal organisations make use of legitimate business for transport facilities, accommodation and money laundering. The Hungarian study mentions contacts with legitimate business primarily in the logistics sectors, such as transportation and accommodation. However, the Hungarian study was limited to one type of organised crime, namely the smuggling of illegal immigrants.

In most Dutch cases, the members of criminal groups had their own companies. This concerned all kinds of businesses, such as import-export firms, restaurants, cafes and travel agencies. Although many of these firms were not directly used as a tool for carrying out criminal activities, they did facilitate them. In most cases, they provided a good cover for transport and a high number of international telephone calls. Moreover, the experiences gained by organising and running a business and trading, were useful for organising their illegal trade. In several other cases the infrastructures of legitimate enterprises served as an effective cover and support for criminal activities. Sometimes legal businesses were set up aimed at facilitating illegal businesses. They served as a cover for the logistics, the flow of money or money laundering activities.

What the case studies demonstrate is the willingness amongst many individuals in the world of legitimate business to ignore or tolerate obvious criminal activities, or even to profit from them as long as the risks involved seem minor. There is considerable complaisance, and many people have the attitude that they want to 'stay out of trouble', 'mind their own business', or sometimes 'give aspiring poor people a break'. These forms of tolerance provide organised criminals with the environment that they require to be able to operate.

3.2 Existing measures

3.2.1 The scope of the administrative approach in general

In literature on organised crime, two forms are distinguished: trade in illegal goods and services, and racketeering in legal markets. Examples of the first category are drug trafficking, woman trafficking and the smuggling of illegal immigrants. Racketeering refers to obtaining or occupying positions of power in certain areas or branches of industry. In certain regions of the US, racketeering activities constitute the majority of organised crime. Since the 1980s, strict criminal law enforcement has led to the incarceration of several top figures of the five *cosa nostra* 'families' in New York city (Jacobs *et al.*, 1999). However, this was not sufficient to remove the presence of criminal organisations from the positions of power they obtained in several branches of industry, e.g. waste processing, the construction industry and food markets such as the Fulton Fish Market in Manhattan. The city's authorities realised that criminal law alone would be inadequate for fighting such monopolies. Several branches of industry in which organised crime was active were subjected to administrative regulation. While the New York mob tried to acquire positions of power in *legal markets*, the core business of criminal organisations in the cases of Finland, Hungary, Italy and the Netherlands lies within *illegal markets*. The main instrument of an administrative approach to organised crime is regulating *legal* markets. It is only when markets are legalised that administrative instruments can be used to expel or to prevent the infiltration of organised crime. For this reason, brothel ownership has been legalised in the Netherlands. With the use of instruments such as permits and inspections, this legalisation is aimed at deterring harmful forms of prostitution, such as prostitution by minors, illegal immigrants and trafficked women. In *illegal* markets, the possibilities of administrative preventive measures are limited. Even in these situations, organised crime groups 'touch' the legitimate world, for example, by setting up legal persons or transferring the proceeds of crime by use of financial institutions. These interfaces between illegitimate and legitimate worlds also offer opportunities for administrative regulation.

3.2.2 The integrity of the public administration

A large number of measures with regard to the prevention of organised crime have been taken over the last fifteen years, both on a European level and a national level. On the one hand, these measures aimed at improving the integrity as well as upgrading the instruments of public administration, in order to prevent its penetration by organised crime. On the other hand, legislation has focused on business itself; with instructions to conduct transactions with greater diligence and report any unusual transactions.

In order to improve the integrity of their public administrations, many countries have worked on tightening up their corruption laws and increasing the maximum penalties. Some countries have initiated major campaigns which were intended to stimulate compliance with the legislation. An example is the 'Clean Hands' investigation of political corruption in Italy, a major operation extending from the lower levels of public administration to the uppermost levels of the political and economic system. Since 1992, the magistracy has uncovered a scene of corruption and political illegality which was unprecedented in the history of western democracy, involving the entire political class of the country and broad sectors of its business community (Della Porta and Vanucci, 1999).[33] For such reasons, it is important that other conditions are met to prevent corruption.

The Hungarian report points out that improving the financial position of public officials and law enforcement personnel – better wages and living standards – is also an important method for preventing the temptation of corruption.

The fact that public administration has been given the tools to prevent abuse in issuing permits, grants or public tenders for criminal purposes is as important as the fight against corruption. A good example of this administrative approach to organised crime is the Italian system of *certificazioni, comunicazioni e informazioni antimafia,* the anti-Mafia warning system (Di Nicola, 2000). Italy is the first country in the European Union where investigations of the antecedents of companies, the so-called *criminal audits,* are regulated by law and systematically conducted on a national level. Because of the seriousness of the organised crime problem in Italy, the *Legislazione antimafia* (anti-Mafia legislation) is wide-reaching. This legislation obliges government bodies to conduct an investigation (or have it conducted) into the criminal background of all tenders and candidates, prior to awarding licenses, permits, concessions, financial allowances, authorisations or the admission of tenders and the conclusion, approval or allowance of different contracts, including tender contracts. Screening is conducted on the basis of information provided by the applicant, from financial institutions, Chambers of Commerce and all governmental databases, including law enforcement agencies. When it is discovered that a criminal court has prohibited a person suspected or convicted of organised crime from contracting with the public administration or that tendering enterprises or corporations are suspected to be under organised crime infiltration, the administration cannot sign a public contract with such persons, enterprises or corporations. (Manunza, 2001; Van Heddeghem *et al.,* 2002).

Following the Italian and New York examples, the Netherlands has also developed an administrative approach to organised crime. The draft bill was passed by Parliament and implemented mid 2003. The new act (*BIBOB* Act) creates a legal basis to refuse or withdraw permits, licences, grants and subsidies when there is a serious threat of abuse by criminals.[34] This decision must be based on a screening and risk assessment of the integrity of the applicant, which is not conducted by the governmental body itself, but by a special agency, the *BIBOB* Bureau, which is located at the Department of Justice. This body also screens participants in public tender procedures for the application of the grounds for exclusion in EU Directives. The purpose of this bureau is to support local public authorities, such as city administrations, municipalities and provinces, in enforcing the law. The bureau has the authority to consult criminal and tax records as well as police

33 The investigation reached the highest levels of public administration and affected most areas of the state's activities. More than 500 former parliamentarians were implicated, many former ministers, five former premiers, thousands of local administrators and public functionaries, the army, the customs service (responsible for investigating financial crimes in general), the main publicly owned companies and even sectors of the magistracy itself. Besides the illegal funding of political parties by private business, the indictments also concerned taking bribes from the Mafia.

34 The scope of the *BIBOB* screening system is limited to certain branches of industry which are considered to be vulnerable to organised crime: hotels and restaurants, the sex industry, construction, waste processing, public housing and transport.

intelligence on organised crime. On the basis of the administrative and financial information, the bureau provides the requesting authority with written advice, in which it indicates the seriousness of the threat of abuse.

3.2.3 The integrity of local businesses

In many areas of business, it has become common practice that corporations and even individuals are required to engage in the systematic 'surveillance' of normal business activities in order to detect and report signs of illegal activity or suspicious transactions.[35] To avoid illegal migration, for example, airlines have stepped up their efforts to ensure that travellers have the proper documentation. In such cases, a system of fines imposed upon the carriers has provided a strong stimulant. A similar process is in development in relation to European truck drivers and to ferry boats serving the British Channel. In the chemical industry within the EU, companies and traders are required to report suspicious transactions involving approximately two dozen chemical products that can be used for the production of illegal narcotics.[36] Suspicious transactions in other unlisted chemical products may be reported on a voluntary basis. An area in which private sector organisations have been very active working against organised crime is that of credit crime, either through various payment cards or through commercial finance.[37] Such initiatives are usually aimed at detecting irregular patterns in credit behaviour, often involving the use of fake or stolen identities.

Preventive action can be focused on individual private companies or on professional, trade and industry associations. Codes of conduct can enhance the integrity of a business sector. Drawing up an explicit set of disciplinary rules setting out the responsibilities of those working in certain business domains can help maintain integrity and expose irregular or outright criminal practices. The transport sector, for obvious reasons, would benefit from the introduction of a code of conduct and disciplinary rules. Additionally, professional associations can contribute to problem awareness by publishing cases of wrongful conduct and outright fraud in their sector, and by pointing out the mechanisms of vulnerability.

Increasingly, corporations and other private entities apply civil law instruments in solving 'horizontal' conflicts. Wrongful acts committed by companies and individual operators involved in criminal schemes can be countered when those who were victimised take their cases to court. Chain liability legislation has been introduced in several European countries to allow for the prosecution

---

35 Home Office Research Development and Statistics Directorate, NCIS, Swedish Crime Prevention Council, Europol (2001), *The Identification, Development and Exchange of Good Practice for Reducing Organised Crime* (draft version March 2001), p. 105.
36 Policy regarding XTC (*Beleid inzake XTC*), *Handelingen II* 2000/01, 23 760, No. 14, pp. 10-11.
37 Home Office Research Development and Statistics Directorate, NCIS, Swedish Crime Prevention Council, Europol (2001), *The Identification, Development and Exchange of Good Practice for Reducing Organised Crime* (draft version March 2001), pp. 113 and 130 ff.

of companies that have indirectly profited from cheap labour through subcontractors, with employees for whom no benefits and taxes were paid. The same legal instrument could be applied in other schemes where companies attempt to avoid responsibility by introducing third parties.

3.3 Best practices

3.3.1 The administrative approach in Amsterdam

An interesting example of preventative measures is the administrative approach to organised crime by the city of Amsterdam. Amsterdam is a well-known centre for the trade of ecstasy, cocaine, heroin and cannabis. Furthermore, for a long time the city has had a policy of tolerance towards certain practices, such as prostitution and the use of soft drugs. In the last decade, criminal organisations have been able to build up positions of economic power in real estate, bars and restaurants, especially in the famous 'Red Light' district in the inner city (Fijnaut et al., 1998: 138). It is highly probable that these positions of power are financed with capital from drug trafficking. In response to this, the city administration set up a special preventive programme to combat organised crime. As a result of this programme, action is being taken on three fronts: firstly, in the integrity of the civil service apparatus, secondly, in the screening of security processes concerning public tender procedures and thirdly, in the infiltration of organised crime in certain areas and branches of industry in the city.

Firstly, a project was set up aimed at creating awareness amongst executives and civil servants on the nature, scope and development of corruption and fraud, and to update them on better ways to master these issues. The most important principle that arose was that an awareness of the risks of criminality should be institutionalised in the entire bureaucratic and political organisation of Amsterdam. This means that in every service or branch concrete action has to be taken (vulnerability analysis; detecting opportunities for corruption and fraud). Finally, a special bureau was set up which is responsible for the further implementation of prevention policies and the investigation of suspected cases of fraud or corruption.

Secondly, screening and security procedures were enacted to prevent companies with criminal connections from participating in public tendering procedures. Screening is conducted by a special agency, the Screening and Audit Bureau (SBA), under the direct authority of the mayor. To carry out its tasks properly, this agency not only uses its own expert analysts but also cooperates closely with the police, the public prosecution service, the fiscal authorities and the municipal services.

Thirdly, a project was set up to chase down organised crime in certain regional areas and economic branches of the city. Initially, this project focused on the notorious Red Light district. After three years of operating successfully, the project expanded to other areas and branches in the city. Some examples of the selected areas are rundown streets in poor areas with a high number of immigrants, the most expensive shopping street in the city and the industrial harbour district. Some examples of the selected branches are the so-called smart shops which may participate in drug trafficking, phone centres which may be used for illegal money transfers and the escort business which may be used for women trafficking. Basically, the project team follows a two-step approach. The first step is the collection and analysis of data on the selected areas or branches. The project team has special authority to collect data from the police, the public prosecution and in some cases the fiscal authorities. Through the combination of this information with data from the municipal authorities, an assessment is made of the presence of organised crime. The second step is to take measures on the basis of this assessment. Besides criminal investigations and fiscal claims, administrative measures can be taken such as the refusal or withdrawal of permits and the closure of certain establishments, for instance when a bar plays a role in drug trafficking. Refusing and withdrawing permits is difficult without the implementation of the *BIBOB* Bill, but existing legislation does offer some possibilities for taking action, such as withdrawing a licence to serve liquor when a bar owner has a criminal record. Finally, the project team also takes civil measures, such as purchasing real estate to prevent it from falling into the hands of criminal organisations.

The project in Amsterdam is an example of a multi-agency approach in which several agencies cooperate by sharing information and integral enforcement (Garland, 1996). Although an evaluation is still in progress, the project in Amsterdam can be considered to be a success. It has created awareness of the threats of organised crime within the civil service, the city and neighbourhood councils, and it has produced results in preventing organised crime infiltrating certain businesses.

3.3.2 Public-private cooperation

The World Customs Organization (WCO) provides an excellent example of successful cooperation between government and private entities. The WCO has initiated and signed a large number of Memoranda of Understanding (MOU) with a range of trade associations and organisations in the transport sector to enhance problem awareness and information exchange regarding the illicit transportation of narcotics (Schneider *et al.*, 2000: 130 ff.).[38] Amongst the partner organisations are the International Air Transport Association (IATA), the Baltic and International Maritime Council (BIMCO) and the International Federation of Freight Forwarders Association. The WCO also encourages and facilitates national Customs agencies to sign MOUs with domestic carriers and companies. In the United States, the US Customs Service has been very active in engaging

38   Home Office Research Development and Statistics Directorate, NCIS, Swedish Crime Prevention Council, Europol (2001), *The Identification, Development and Exchange of Good Practice for Reducing Organised Crime* (draft version March 2001), p. 112 ff.

in various partnerships with the private sector through the Carrier Initiative Program, amongst others, in which the vast majority of corporations in the transport industry are signatories. In 1996, the US private sector started its own voluntary programme to screen business processes to deter narcotic traffickers, entitled the Business Anti-Smuggling Coalition (BASC). The International Chamber of Commerce is currently working on expanding BASC around the world. In 1999 in Europe, the European Commission and Europol initiated a move towards a comprehensive strategy to combat transnational organised crime through a coordinated, multi-sectored forum involving the law enforcement sector, the criminal justice system, regulatory agencies, the private sector, academia and public administration (Schneider *et al.*, 2000: 128 ff).

3.3.3 Security Main port Rotterdam

It is obviously not necessary to wait until an organised crime problem openly and forcefully manifests itself in a full-blown form for action to be taken. Using risk assessment tools such as the method proposed by Albanese (2001), governments and others can devise an early warning system which will alert them to any possible developing threats and enable them to put preventive measures in place on time.

Specifying the role of various participants in the logistical chain of a seaport, for example, and linking them to the specific criminal risks involved, will help to target organised crime control efforts in the port of Rotterdam (Brink, 2002: 127-129). In Rotterdam, a platform of crime control has been established in order to reduce the crime risks in the port and risks for businesses unwittingly becoming involved in illegal activities. Participants are the relevant businesses in the harbour and state agencies, such as the police, customs, public prosecutor and various municipal agencies.

Together they aim to increase the awareness of all parties in the main port and their activities are not limited to merely offering vague advice.[39] In 2000, a guidebook was produced entitled Security Main port Rotterdam.[40] The guide examines security management in general and the risks in business processes, personnel management, finances, information technology and computerisation, and company grounds and premises. Furthermore, a survey describing the most important logistic chains in Rotterdam harbour and the role of the most important private parties (conveyers, ship owners, ship-brokers, stevedores, insurers, bankers, etc.) has been drawn up. The vulnerability for crime is described and analysed according to three aspects of logistics: the data flow, the movements of goods and the flow of money. Finally, the guide gives recommendations for decreasing vulnerability and crime risks.

---

39   The complete guide as well as other information can be found at http://www.portofrotterdam.com (dd. 29 April 2003).

40   *Regionaal Platform Criminaliteitsbeheersing Rotterdam, Regionaal Platform voor de Rotterdamse Haven & Industrie* (2000), *Security Main port Rotterdam: een betrouwbare logistieke keten, Rotterdam: Platform Criminaliteitbeheersing Rotterdam* (also available at http://www.portofrotterdam.com (dd. 29 April 2003).

Late 2003, a revised version of the guide will be published. This will be entitled the PSD Toolkit (Port Security Development Toolkit). This Guide is being developed "as a pro-active practical and transparent computerized security instrument". A self-assessment is included in the guide which enables businesses to enhance their insight into relevant crime and terrorist risks, and to analyse the extent to which security measures have been established.

3.3.4 Behind the facades of legal persons

In several countries, the authorities have devised ways to supervise legal entities such as limited companies as well as private individuals for fraud prevention purposes. Among other things, this concerns the screening, monitoring and auditing of companies and branches, and establishing and maintaining registers of bankruptcies and trade bans. To a large extent, these measures have not been specially established to prevent organised crime, but they are considered to be possible tools for that purpose (Seger, 2003: 10, 14). However, this is not always the case. Within the framework of the preventive policy against organised crime in the Netherlands, measures on the supervision of natural and legal persons have been adjusted and supplementary measures have been taken. At the Dutch ministry of Justice, the Business Integrity Department and the Legal Persons Division of the Central Organisation for Certificates Concerning Behaviour apply a range of methods to increase the transparency of legal persons and the integrity of the business world. In 1998, the '*Vennoot*' database system was set up to bring together relevant data on legal entities for crime prevention purposes. This database contains information on the identity of all those involved in setting up new limited companies or altering their statutes. It also includes bankruptcies and suspensions of payments as pronounced by the courts. The database is also used for investigative purposes and new data sources are constantly being made available to the Central Organisation for Certificates Concerning Behaviour. The establishment of such a preventive policy does have its limitations. Firstly, as the Finish report illustrates, the business community distrust measures in the economic field as it can strengthen the position of the government and increase bureaucracy. The growing awareness of unfair competition and running the risk of financial losses would increase the acceptance of these preventive measures. Secondly, to execute these kinds of preventive measures there is a need for intensive cooperation and the exchange of information on a national and international level. These issues are certainly important regarding the level playing field and achieving open competition on a European level. According to Seger (2003: 21), a crime preventive policy is a valid reason for different ministries to exchange information and cooperate on both a national and international level.

3.4   Conclusions and recommendations

Criminal organisations try to corrupt public and law enforcement officials and make use of legitimate businesses to facilitate their criminal operations. The interfaces between organised crime and the legitimate world pose a threat to the integrity of this world, while simultaneously contributing to the continued existence of organised crime. However, these interfaces also provide many starting points for crime prevention and as such, they constitute the chief weaknesses in the perpetuation of organised crime. This chapter has focused on the essential values of the awareness of public administrations and businesses about the risks imposed by organised crime. In addition, it has demonstrated the importance of creating a level of integrity which would enable public administrations and businesses to reject any suspicious interactions with the criminal environment.

However, creating such a level of awareness requires a great deal of effort. It is nevertheless worthwhile realising that prevention policy can only be successful when businesses and governments possess a sufficient level of integrity, a necessary condition for the effective prevention of organised crime. The growth of awareness and integrity are therefore highly important. It is characteristic of the abovementioned four best practices that they focus on sharing information, improve cooperation and attempt to foster consciousness regarding public and commercial interests in preventing organised crime. Awareness can be increased through legislation. If businesses are held responsible for contracting illegal subcontractors or if they risk being involved in a criminal or civil lawsuit for, for example, failing to perform sound pre-boarding checks, they will obviously develop a greater level of awareness.

The first step is to create and maintain a high level of awareness of the possible abuse of public services and to use the existing tools to prevent this. The Finnish national report gives a good example of this first basic step. The report points out that, as renting or buying real estate constitutes a considerable facilitating factor for organised crime and an important bridge between legal and illegal activities, some interventions are possible and relatively easily to put into effect. In the case of immigrants residing in welfare service flats, there is usually the situation that people are completely unaware of the rules regarding the use of the flats by third parties. Simply increasing information about these restrictions and related sanctions would restrict a decent number of potential facilitators from storerooms. In addition, social welfare authorities could keep a more effective check on the actual use of welfare service accommodation.

In this, a central issue is obtaining and sharing information, although the effectiveness of prevention depends on obtaining all the relevant information. Administrative authorities therefore have to create protocols and procedures for managing applications and in addition, they need to have an information system which is supplied with all the relevant information. With regard to databases, those with information on legal persons are examples of good practises. However, in order to obtain relevant information one is usually dependent on other authorities. The Amsterdam project demonstrates that the police and tax department may be reluctant to provide the administrative authorities with criminal intelligence. Information should not only be relevant, but also reliable. In general, it is difficult to acquire reliable evidence on organised crime. The use of criminal intelligence and information from the police is crucial, but even then it is often hard to create a link to organised crime. For an administrative authority, it is even harder to evaluate the reliability of police information. In the Italian anti-Mafia system and the Dutch *BIBOB* system, a conviction is not necessary and a criminal suspicion is sufficient. But what if the information proves to be false and the person is later acquitted? In the Dutch system there is a risk of claims: the administrative authority is liable for any damages incurred if a permit or a project has not been granted based on false information.

Because of these limitations and conditions, obtaining, analysing and assessing information on connections to organised crime with the aim of taking administrative measures, requires a huge amount of expertise. Moreover, privacy regulations means that there are limitations to the extent that public authorities may consult confidential databases. For this reason, a recommendation may be to have a special agency undertake this complicated task.

Awareness, integrity and reliable information are thus essential ingredients in effective prevention. Though existing legislation and authoritative powers already offer great potential, there is a need for implementing appropriate legal instruments. For example, if the available measures are not sufficient to stop the criminal use of legitimate business, extra authoritative powers and instruments for screening, risk assessment and excluding businesses from public services should be put in place. The Amsterdam project has the authority to consult criminal records for information on criminal connections, but as long as the *BIBOB* bill was not in operation, the city had no legal grounds to use this information as a means of excluding criminals from governmental services. With all the new strategies to fight organised crime, we should be aware of any undesirable side effects. For instance, the intensified inspection of goods and persons by customs and border police will increase the need and therefore the risk of corruption for these officials to admit illegal goods or persons. Furthermore, a pre-qualification procedure is not a panacea for preventing the criminal infiltration of branches of industry. A number of conditions are mandatory for such a procedure to work properly. This includes insights by the relevant services regarding the structure and workings of the industry, and linked to this, insights regarding the quality of the questionnaire. The amount of information available by the person checking the answers is also relevant. Indeed, if these preconditions are not fulfilled, this sort of procedure could have an opposite effect in that it could legitimise companies which rightfully should not have met the requirements (Fijnaut, 2002). Other side effects which could be expected are counter strategies by criminal organisations. When applicants for permits or the participation in tender procedures are screened, they may use foreign legal entities which are more difficult to screen. This phenomenon has already been observed in Amsterdam.

4 Legal professions

Hans Nelen and Francien Lankhorst[41]

The four national reports contain several red flags in terms of members of the legal profession who act as a bridge between organised crime and the legitimate world. Various cases were presented in which lawyers, notaries, real estate agents, tax consultants, accountants or other professionals were somehow connected to criminal activities. In this chapter we will focus on the delicate role certain professionals play in shielding crimes and criminal proceeds from the authorities. We will restrict ourselves to the position and role of lawyers. The relationship between a lawyer and client is a special one which is protected by a legally stipulated duty to maintain confidentiality and the privilege of non-disclosure to any third parties (including judges).

Firstly, we will discuss some risk factors that may lead to lawyers improperly assisting organised criminal groups. Secondly, the services rendered by lawyers which are subject to abuse by criminal networks will be highlighted. Some aspects of the culpable involvement of lawyers in the activities of criminal networks will be presented. This survey is based on the case studies of the four national reports and the analysis of relevant critical studies.

After describing some risk factors and aspects of culpable involvement, the emphasis will then be placed on finding ways which could ultimately benefit the legal profession in preventing excessive involvement with criminals. The existing repressive and preventive measures will also be discussed briefly. At the end of the chapter we will suggest a limited number of new preventive measures which could possibly improve and extend the existing approach. We refer to the current research *Dilemma's facing the legal professions in their professional relationships with 'criminal' clients* for a more detailed analysis.[42]

4.1 Risk factors and key problems

Theoretically, the combination of financial and legal knowledge and the aura of respectability and reliability make lawyers attractive potential partners for organised crime. After all, they are in the position of offering legal advice in court and can provide the expertise required to launder criminal proceeds. For

41 Hans Nelen is lecturer at the Department of Criminology at the Vrije Universiteit of Amsterdam and Francien Lankhorst is PhD candidate at the same department.

42 This is also an international comparative study which is being conducted in four countries - the Netherlands, Italy, the United Kingdom and France - focusing on the issues of compromising conduct, the privilege of non-disclosure and professional secrecy. The principal aim of this research - which is supervised by Nelen and Lankhorst at the Institute of Criminology at the Vrije Universiteit Amsterdam, the Netherlands - is to gain a better insight into the dilemmas affecting the integrity of members of the legal profession, notaries and the existing supervising codes and regulations. Particular emphasis is placed on the dilemmas regarding the possibility of becoming involved in organised crime and the measures lawyers and notaries must take in order to prevent such involvement without it having a negative effect on the characteristics specific to their occupation i.e. professional secrecy and client confidentiality. The study is also co-financed by the European Commission in the context of the Falcone programme and will be completed in the summer of 2003.

the outside world, the participation of a lawyer in a transaction can create the impression of legitimacy. From the perspective of the criminal network, the most important beneficial aspect of working with a lawyer is the confidential nature of the relationship and the privilege of non-disclosure. This is the main reason why the interactions between lawyers, their clients and associates are inherently non-transparent.

The four national reports demonstrate that lawyers are able to assist the illegal behaviour of their clients and organised criminal groups in various ways, and that they have the potential to inflict (and indeed have inflicted) significant damage on the profession's reputation. The most striking examples can be found in the Italian and Dutch national reports. Before we highlight the chief findings of the various national reports, it has to be emphasised that there is little empirical evidence demonstrating the *scale* of the problem. The number of criminal investigations and prosecutions of lawyers is very low. Any conclusions on the extent of the problem would be merely speculative, so we will therefore concentrate on the nature and seriousness of the problem.

An important question is what may be considered to be compromising conduct or the culpable involvement of lawyers. In our definition, compromising conduct exists in two forms. Firstly, professionals can be involved in punishable acts in such a way that they can be criminally prosecuted. They can aid and abet the punishable acts of criminal networks, or facilitate them, for example by fencing or screening stolen goods or by obstructing the investigation of criminal activities or the assets accruing from them. This would be the narrow sense of compromising conduct or culpable involvement. Secondly, compromising conduct or culpable involvement exists in a broad sense if professionals fail to exercise due care in preventing the misuse of their professional capacity for criminal purposes. This does not necessarily imply conscious and deliberate collaboration resulting in criminal offences, but they may be reproached because they could or should have known that their services were being wrongfully used for criminal purposes. It must be clear that the standard of due care goes beyond what is punishable by criminal law. In this report we will focus on both manifestations of compromising conduct.

The first type of culpable involvement distinguished in this study pertains to lawyers who take the notion of partiality to extremes and who serve as a mailbox or errand boy for members of a criminal network. They provide practical help, based on insider knowledge and the assumption of trustworthiness: they transfer letters from their clients in prison to other members of the criminal organisation or they supply confidential file information to unauthorised third parties.

A second manifestation of culpable involvement relates to the intimidation or manipulation of witnesses. Lawyers may do this themselves or they may be aware that other participants of the criminal network are probably harassing witnesses. A somewhat more sophisticated form of assistance other than the abovementioned is when lawyers provide legal advice, credibility and facilities. The case studies demonstrate that legal advice on marriages of convenience may be very important for criminals involved in the trafficking of women. Cases in which lawyers give criminals ample opportunities to use the facilities of the law firm – phone, fax, e-mail – to communicate with each other are also worthy of note. From a criminal's point of view, this is a perfect instrument for shielding criminal activities. After all, both criminals and lawyers are well aware of the legal thresholds and the reluctance amongst police officers and magistrates to use special investigative powers against law firms.

The last example emphasises the fact that the notion of a lawyer as a person who defends a client's case in court, is far too limited. The professional scope of lawyers is tremendously wide and the services they provide are manifold. It is, therefore, a misconception that most cases of compromising conduct refer to criminal defence practitioners. Naturally, they do play a part in some types of culpable involvement, but in general, most cases predominantly relate to lawyers specialised in civil law. This finding reflects a number of changes within the profession in recent decades, such as the increasing level of commercialisation, mergers, takeovers and fierce competition within the ranks of the profession.

In addition to the representation of clients in and out of court and providing legal advice, a large number of lawyers are increasingly tending to engage in other commercial activities. They may create corporate and trust entities (in mainstream jurisdictions and abroad), act as a manager of these entities, open a bank account or conduct financial transactions on behalf of clients etc. The distinction – in terms of commercial activities – between these types of lawyers and other professionals, such as tax consultants and other financial and legal specialists, has diminished somewhat in recent decades. The major differences which remain are lawyer/client confidentiality and the privilege of non-disclosure. These characteristics make lawyers specialised in civil law an attractive means for organised crime to enter the legitimate economy.

In all the national reports, the cases suggest that the most important reason why criminals turn to a lawyer is the associated need to store and use the proceeds of crime without running any risks. This finding is in line with several reports from the Financial Action Task Force on Money Laundering, which have determined that the involvement of lawyers and other professionals in laundering is a matter of concern.[43] The FATF Report on Money Laundering Typologies, published in 2001, identified the following forms of assistance:[44]

- Creating corporate vehicles or other complex legal arrangements such as trusts;
- Buying or selling property;
- Performing financial transactions;
- Offering financial and tax advice;
- Providing introductions to financial institutions.

Other services lawyers are known to have provided in suspicious circumstances are:
- Receiving cash;
- Providing the client or the client's associates with cash;

43 Financial Action Task Force on Money Laundering (1999a) sections 136, (1999b) 47, (2001) 31-37 and (2002) 272-280.
44 Financial Action Task Force on Money Laundering (2001) section 33.

- Paying monies to third parties in 'transactions' not connected with the lawyer's underlying retainer;
- Passing money through their own personal or business accounts;
- Assisting criminals to run their laundering activities from prison.

In a number of cases that were studied in the context of this research project, the lawyer is involved in a chain of financial transactions and provides several of the aforementioned services. They not only store considerable amounts of money on behalf of their clients, but they also pass money through their own personal or business accounts to other accounts, and conceive complex financial constructions to mislead the judicial and fiscal authorities.
In some of the cases, a shift in the role that the lawyer plays within the criminal network may be observed. They initially function as an external expert who is engaged by the criminal network to perform certain duties, but gradually they become more and more involved, both commercially and socially. They may join the leading members at social events – parties, football matches etc. – and regularly and consciously perform all kind of services for them. A good illustration of this is a drugs case in which the two main important experts were a lawyer and a legal advisor. The former advised the leading members of the criminal group on a regular basis. He had his own licit legal practice, which was located in the office complex of one the leading members of the network.

4.2 Existing measures

During the last decade, government agencies have increasingly taken steps against the legal profession by means of new laws and guidelines to curtail professional behaviour and combat unacceptable links with criminals. Anti-money laundering laws have been tightened and the activities of lawyers have come under the scope of new legislation. In the Netherlands, for example, lawyers may be prosecuted on the basis of article 420*bis* of the Criminal Code. This article not only covers the areas of deliberate and habitual laundering, but also contains a section which deals with negligent laundering. The latter is particularly important for lawyers as it stipulates that "a person shall be guilty of negligent laundering and liable to a prison sentence of up to one year or a fine in category five if:

a   he disguises or conceals the real nature, source, location, disposal or movement of the subject matter, or disguises or conceals who the legal owner of the subject matter is, or keeps possession of the subject matter and ought reasonably to suspect that it has been directly or indirectly derived from a criminal act;

b   he acquires, keeps possession of, transfers or makes use of the revenue from the subject matter, and ought reasonably to suspect that it has been directly or indirectly derived from a criminal act."

This legislation is rather new (2002) and to date no lawyer has been prosecuted on the basis of this article. As stated above, prosecutions and convictions of lawyers are generally rare, not only in the Netherlands but also in Italy, Hungary and Finland. Nevertheless, representative bodies of lawyers have certainly been taking the issue of professional integrity more into account. They tend to emphasise the need for self-regulation. In several countries, national Bar associations have introduced new guidelines according to which lawyers have an obligation to examine the purpose of a client's request if they suspect that their services might be subject to abuse. It remains unclear, however, how far-reaching this obligation is.

In practice, the effects of vetting clients and anti-laundering measures depend not only on the morality and financial circumstances of professionals, but also on the perception of the risk and results of detection: this in turn depends on the nature of the rules governing behaviour and the level of compliance to these rules. Levels of *visible* enforcement of these provisions have been extremely modest in Europe.

This brings us to the role that disciplinary boards play in investigating lawyers and imposing disciplinary measures on those who violate the rules of integrity. In all four countries, relatively few cases of culpable involvement have been brought before disciplinary boards. One explanation for the limited power of disciplinary boards is that proceedings are generally instituted by parties with a direct interest in the case. The accessibility of outsiders – such as law enforcement agencies and public prosecutors – is limited. Another relevant factor is that these organisations do not have investigative facilities, nor do they have the facilities to monitor the individual conduct of their members. Up until now, the "self-cleansing" capacity of professional organisations by means of disciplinary action has transpired to be very limited (also see Fijnaut *et al.*, 1998).

4.3 Possible preventive measures

A recent directive of the European Commission best illustrates the discussion regarding the legal profession.[45] This directive stipulates that Member States should compel their legal professionals – amongst others – to report any unusual or suspicious financial transactions to the appropriate authorities. Notably, this has far-reaching implications for certain specific professional rights, such as lawyer/client confidentiality and the privilege of non-disclosure.

Not surprisingly, for a long time members of the legal profession have been strongly opposed to such an obligation and they have in fact felt that they were being forced to act as an investigative authority. According to representatives of several lawyers' associations, such a development would be in clear

---

45 Directive 2001/97/EC of the European Parliament and the Council of 4 December 2001, amending Council Directive 91/308/EEC on the prevention of the use of the financial system for the purpose of money laundering, *OJ L 344*, 28/12/01, 76.

contravention with the unique function lawyers fulfil in modern society and the specific professional rights with which they are equipped to enable them to function as such. However, the atrocities in the USA on 11 September 2001 fundamentally changed the situation and stifled the opposition of all professional groups, including lawyers: long-running negotiations on the money laundering directive were quickly concluded in the latter part of that year and lawyers were clearly brought within anti-money laundering laws. The question is what will be the effect of this new obligation to report unusual or suspect transactions. At this stage, the answer to this question is merely speculative, as in most countries the European Commission's new directive still has to be implemented in national legislation and carried out in daily practice. What we do know, however, is that up until now the way law enforcement agencies have used information on suspicious financial transactions is not very promising, at least this is the case in the Netherlands. The system of the disclosure of unusual transactions dates back to the beginning of the 1990s. In 2001, the Dutch Financial Intelligence Unit (the Centre for reporting unusual transactions; MOT),[46] registered a record of 76,085 unusual transactions. About one quarter of these were labelled 'suspicious' and were consequently transferred to the police. However, due to a lack of organisational facilities, manpower, expertise and, above all, interest, valuable financial information does not receive adequate attention in the process of law enforcement. Only a tiny percentage of reports of suspicious transactions are actually followed up. There is no evidence whatsoever that the extension of the obligation to report certain financial transactions to other professional groups will lead to more – and, in particular, more successful – law enforcement.[47]

The findings of this study suggest that a regulatory approach to the facilitation of wrongdoing by lawyers is likely to be more effective than a law enforcement approach, because, unlike law enforcement agencies, regulators may:

- routinely inspect confidential and privileged material and thus both monitor compliance and uncover serious wrongdoing;
- better assess the behaviour of lawyers;
- take preventative steps such as intervention;
- undertake regulatory incapacitation by suspension or by expulsion;
- conduct all of the above well before any criminal case could come to trial.

The fact that up until now the power of the disciplinary boards has been rather limited, demonstrates that self-regulation on its own is inadequate. It would therefore be worthwhile considering not only expanding the executive powers of administrative supervisory boards – to enable them to investigate the questionable behaviour of lawyers more thoroughly and, if necessary, impose severe administrative sanctions – but also stimulating law enforcement

---

46 legislation on the disclosure of unusual transactions came into force on 1 February 1994.

47 Research by Terlouw and Aron (1996) showed that during the first few years, only 3% of the reported *unusual* transactions were used for law enforcement purposes. The number of reports has accelerated, but the capacity of the authorities to process them has not kept pace, so the current percentage is unlikely to be any higher.

agencies to pay more attention to professionals who render services to criminals. A mixture of an administrative and law enforcement approach is, in terms of both a repressive and preventive strategy, the best option. The process of paying more attention to the professional integrity of lawyers will benefit from such a multi-dimensional approach, as all participants will become more aware of the necessity of improving mutual cooperation and the exchange of information.

4.4 Best practices

Lawyers are inclined to emphasise the need for both autonomy and partiality in practising their profession. The element of autonomy is reflected in the rules of conduct which stipulate that entanglements of interests due to financial or personal relationships should be avoided. The aspect of partiality implies that the specific interests of a client are more important than the general interests of society. As illustrated above, in some circumstances lawyers run the risk of upsetting the balance between autonomy and partiality. They become involved in a situation where they are too dependent on their clients and are merely the amoral executors of the clients' wishes.

This imbalance may be rectified by stimulating the debate amongst lawyers on professional ethics and integrity. One professional norm, formulated in the Netherlands to safeguard lawyers' autonomy, stipulates that they should refuse to take a case if the case conflicts with their sense of justice. This guiding principle is rather broadly formulated. After all, there is no general consensus on norms and values amongst lawyers. From an ethical point of view, the same case may be acceptable to one lawyer and totally unacceptable to another. Nevertheless, it is possible – and desirable – to design professional rules according to which lawyers are prevented from behaving in compromising ways in relation to organised crime. This is particularly important in the context of an anti-money laundering strategy. As we have seen, lawyers who are specialised in civil law particularly run the risk of becoming involved in money-laundering schemes. According to the 'know your customer' principle, a professional standard might stipulate that lawyers (specialised in civil law) when taking a case, must consider who the client is, what the clients wants, whether the request is unusual and why they have been chosen to perform these particular services. If lawyers are still in doubt whether or not to render their services after such a preliminary 'investigation', they should be able to consult a confidant for professional advice. In the Netherlands, a system of confidants or 'trusted representatives' already exists within the organisation of public notaries. It may be worthwhile implementing such a system within the legal profession as a whole.

Once lawyers decide to refuse or return a case because of suspicious circumstances, it would be highly beneficial if their colleagues were informed of the reasons for their decision. Modern communication technology means that it is easy to disseminate information about questionable cases amongst the members of professional organisations and, in particular, to inform them about the *modus operandi* of criminals who try to abuse the services of the legal profession. Naturally, lawyer/client confidentiality has to be taken into account here. If necessary, the option of anonymous case descriptions may be considered.

4.5   Conclusions and recommendations

During the last decade, both on a national and international level, there has been a public debate regarding the compromising conduct of the legal profession and the possible measures which could be taken against such conduct. This study shows that the evidence of the abuse of legal professional privilege and client confidentiality stems from incidental cases, rather than there being any clear empirical trend or statistical basis. Given the nature of the problem, this is not surprising. After all, social scientists reproduce the blind spots of law enforcement officials, because they face the same problem: the privileges of confidentiality and non-disclosure operate as a very effective barrier to initiating enquiries and this can only be overcome by strong evidence from other sources. Although the number of cases of the culpable involvement of lawyers is rather low, the case studies and interviews in the four national reports contain several indications that:
- The specific features of the legal profession make it attractive for some criminals to involve lawyers in their activities, notably the financial and reputable credibility that a lawyer's involvement can provide;
- The legal professional privilege and confidentiality provide frontline protection against investigation; and
- The legitimate private interactions between lawyers and clients generate a cloak under which dishonest relationships can be concealed.

Trends towards ever-increasing commercialisation, internationalisation and cooperation with other disciplines may have a negative impact on the transparency of the activities of the legal profession. Lawyers clearly have discovered markets for legal services beyond the traditional ones and, along with other legal and financial specialists from the same firm, are increasingly acting as advisers or consultants. Some lawyers no longer appear in court and the fundamental question may be raised whether they should still be entitled to have access to all the specific privileges of the discipline.
The issue of lawyer/client confidentiality should be challenged in the light of the changing role that lawyers play in society. Absolute confidentiality seems to be clearly disproportionate in certain circumstances. Although legal confidentiality is and should remain a fundamental right, mechanisms should be installed to ensure that lawyers are accountable and that their dishonest clients cannot abuse confidentiality to shield their illegal behaviour. It is important to stipulate the circumstances under which office accounts, written and oral communication etc. fall under lawyer/client confidentiality. Distinctions based on the nature of the work done for the client might be helpful in this context. Confidentiality

should be strongest in genuine criminal defence paradigm case and weaker where the information being protected relates to a business transaction.

The question is whether such a theoretical distinction in activities is applicable in the daily practice of the legal profession. Lawyers are inclined to argue that a thin line can be drawn between a business consultation on the one hand and legal advice on the other, as it is quite possible that their business consultation may eventually lead to a civil law suit and a court appearance. More research is necessary to find out whether this situation is tenable.

The findings of this study suggest that a regulatory approach to the facilitation of wrongdoing by lawyers is likely to be more effective than a law enforcement approach alone. A mixed strategy would appear to be the best option. Regulators may consider extending their investigatory capacities in order to be able to more accurately assess the behaviour of lawyers, monitor compliance and uncover serious wrongdoing. Consideration should also be given to imposing professional, criminal or administrative sanctions on lawyers who improperly claim the protection of legal professional privilege for their clients.

In several countries, the absence of specific professional rules designed to prevent lawyers from behaving in ways which could facilitate money laundering is rather worrying. After all, one of the most important reasons why criminals engage lawyers is because they need to launder the proceeds of crime. In the context of self-regulation, the formulation of a professional standard should be stimulated in order to prevent lawyers from behaving in compromising ways in relation to money laundering. If lawyers are hesitant about accepting a case from clients, they also need more back up from their own professional organisation. The introduction of confidants or 'trusted representatives' within the various law associations may not only be helpful to individual lawyers who are facing a complex dilemma, but it may also stimulate the debate on professional ethics within the professional organisation in general.

Another area where action could be taken is the dissemination of knowledge amongst members of the legal profession on the *modus operandi* of criminals who try to abuse the services of the legal profession. The description of the patterns of abuse of legal services and the culpable involvement of lawyers may increase the awareness amongst lawyers that their professional capacities may be misused for criminal purposes.

5 Official and informal financial services

Henk van de Bunt and Aljen van Dijken[48]

The anti-money laundering effort has been a cornerstone of the fight against
organised crime since the late 1980s. The fundamental objective of this effort is to
ensure that criminal misuse of the financial system is detected and eradicated.
Since the terrorist attacks in 2001, the financing of terrorism has taken on a new
urgency. This development has given new impulses to the fight against the
misuse of the financial system. In fact, combating organised crime and terrorism
would seem to go hand in hand. The recent FATF report on money laundering
typologies states that "there is little difference in the methods used by terrorist
groups or criminal organisations in attempting to hide or obscure the link
between the source of the funds and their eventual destination or purpose"
(FATF, 2003). However, it is questionable whether the fight against terrorism and
organised crime should be lumped together. Nevertheless, the strong focus on
the fight against terrorism has revitalised the efforts put into controlling the
integrity of the financial sector.

This chapter will not deal with the whole spectrum of anti-money laundering
activities. Rather, it will focus on a vital phase of the money laundering process:
transferring funds from one country to another. There are several methods of
transferring money. Couriers can transport money physically across borders
but this is neither the fastest nor the safest way. A more conventional means
of transferring the proceeds of crime is by using official banks. Though still
appropriated for criminal purposes, anti-money laundering legislation has made
the criminal use of official financial channels less safe. From the perspective
of the perpetrators, transferring money through banks leaves hazardous paper
trails. The party sending the money and the beneficiary both need a bank
account; depositing the money and its transfer are registered. It is therefore
important to focus on two alternative remittance systems. Firstly, we will discuss
money transfer systems which are executed by legitimate non-banking financial
institutions (section 5.1). Secondly, we will look at the opportunities the illicit
environment offers for transferring funds from one country to another. In this
chapter, the use and misuse of *informal money or value transfer systems*
('underground banking') will be described (section 5.2). After both issues have
been introduced, their misuse and any possible countermeasures will be
considered.

5.1 Money Transfer Systems

A money or value transfer service refers to a financial service which accepts cash,
cheques or other valuable goods (diamonds, gold) at one location and pays a

---

48 Henk van de Bunt is Professor in Criminology at Erasmus University Rotterdam and the Vrije Universiteit
Amsterdam and Aljen van Dijken is working at the Department of Criminology at the Vrije Universiteit
Amsterdam.

corresponding sum in cash or another form of remuneration at another location. This takes place by means of a form of communication, a transfer or through a clearing network to which the money or value transfer service belongs. This service may be provided by official banks or by non-banking financial institutions. We will now consider the latter.

MoneyGram and Western Union Money Transfer are the only non-banking official companies which currently offer licit money transfer systems worldwide. Their networks are extensive: MoneyGram has 80,000 service points throughout the world in almost 150 countries[49] and Western Union has agents in approximately 100,000 locations in almost 200 countries across the world.[50]

Through money transfer systems, money can be transferred worldwide, usually in 10 minutes. These financial services have two main advantages: they are fast and easy. The users do not have to use a bank account number. The sender does not have to name the location of the office where the money will be claimed. The recipient is free to choose the service point for receiving the money. A disadvantage of this fast and easy service is, however, the relatively high costs of an individual money transfer. The sending party has to pay the fee and for the smallest amount ($1 – 100) the fee is $12 and for the largest amount ($7,500 – 9,000) the fee is $300.[51] An important aspect of a money transfer is that money has to be delivered and claimed in cash. The transaction costs also have to be paid in cash. Additionally, the users have to provide identification to the agent and both the *sender* as well as the *recipient* are obliged to comply with this condition. Senders have to submit information about their own identity and that of the recipient. They receive a receipt on paper and a unique reference number (MCTN: money transfer control number). This information is electronically stored in a central database of the company's headquarters. The sender must pass the MCTN onto the recipient, which usually is done via a mobile telephone call and this information is required by the recipient in order to claim the money.

However, it would seem that MoneyGram is prepared to deliver money to recipients, even if they do not have identification documents. In an Internet document, MoneyGram states: "[The sending party] can include a test question (something only you and your receiver would know the answer to) on the send transaction. This can serve as an identification method for most transactions below a certain dollar amount".[52] Likewise, Western Union allows recipients to claim money without formal identification documents, if they are able to identify themselves by valid photo identification.[53] MoneyGram cannot offer this particular service in every country as it is dependant on national legislation.[54]

---

49   http://www.gwk.nl/pr_ce.htm
50   http://www.postkantoren.nl/website/topnav/main/postbank/moneytransfer.html
51   These are the MoneyGram fees, http://www.kocbank.com.tr.
52   It is not specified which amounts can be transferred without identification. Generally it is stated that "additional identification and information may be required over certain amounts" http://kocbank.com.tr.
53   Additional identification is needed above certain amounts, http://www.westernunion.com/info.
54   In the Netherlands, the recipient must submit official identification documents to the money transfer service provider.

5.1.1 Misuse of money transfer services

Money transfer systems are useful for migrants to send money to relatives in their homeland, and more incidentally, for persons whose relatives are tourists abroad and who are urgently in need of money. Inevitably, this fast and easy means of sending funds from one country to another worldwide is also attractive for criminals. It is likely that some criminals mistakenly seem to assume that money transfers do not leave a trail and are not reported to the investigative and financial intelligence units.[55] MoneyGram's Internet document would certainly seem to suggest this. In any case, the combination of low-level accessibility (no bank account needed) and the methodology – provision through a unique code in a computer system – provides a fast and relatively anonymous means for channelling funds.

The Italian report mentions several cases in which money was transferred by money transfer services. In one case a money transfer system was even created by the criminal network to transfer huge amounts to Switzerland. In several other cases licit money transfer systems were used for criminal purposes. It has been suggested that the absence of adequate controls on money transfers in some countries heavily damages the controls on international money laundering. One of the red flags in the Italian licit environment is the vulnerability of non-banking financial institutes (e.g. Western Union Money Transfers) for criminal use. In several Finnish cases, the proceeds of crime were transferred by using couriers, money exchange offices and money transfer offices. Several of the criminal networks which were analysed used Estonian owned money transfer offices to transfer illegally earned money to Estonia and elsewhere. By using code numbers and not using the names and addresses of customers these offices could transfer amounts without leaving traces of the senders and recipients. It has been suggested that registration systems and security standards for money transfer services should be designed; bureaus should be required to meet these standards in order to remain in the money transfer business. In the Hungarian report, no reference is made to money transfer services. Only one case provided some information about money laundering in general. In two Dutch cases, money transfer services were used for criminal purposes. In one of these cases, Nigerian women traffickers sent amounts from Holland to Nigeria either by physical transportation or through money transfer services supplied by non-banking institutions. In the other case, a worldwide operating network of smugglers of illegal immigrants used a variety of channels to transfer money. The smugglers and their clients made use of international money transfers by banks and non-banks. Moreover, a network of 'underground bankers' was involved in transferring money between Canada, the Netherlands and Iran, the latter being the smuggled persons' country of origin.

Data from the Dutch Financial Intelligence Unit suggest that the criminal use of

---

55 This perception is not wholly unjustified. One of the Dutch case studies shows that a transaction that should have been reported to the Financial Intelligence Unit, was not.

money transfer services by non-banks still takes place. In 2001, the Unit reported more than 10,500 suspicious money transfers to the police. The three most popular countries of destination were Nigeria (697), Turkey (532) and the Dutch Antilles (488) (*Meldpunt Ongebruikelijke Transacties*, 2002: 33). Suspicious money transfers sent *to* the Netherlands mostly came from Italy (1,042), the United States (902) and Germany (515).

In the case of the trafficking by the Nigerian women, three perpetrators sent amounts to Nigeria more than 600 times (at a total value of at least 120,000 euros). The money transfer offices did not report any of these transactions, despite the fact that a large number of them met the criteria for reporting. This example indicates a weak spot in the fight against money laundering: monitoring and reporting are entrusted (under the threat of sanctions) to the financial institutions who obviously have a commercial interest in not reporting. Compared to the direct contacts between customers and financial service agents on a street level, a great gulf exists between governmental regulatory agencies and money transfer offices.

5.1.2 Counter measures

The FATF has recently developed a 'special recommendation VI' (FATF, 2003). Its objective is to bring all money or value transfer agencies (including 'underground bankers') within the ambit of the anti-money laundering regulations which already exist for the banking sector. According to the FATF, jurisdictions should require the licensing or registration of natural and/or legal persons which provide money or value transfer services. They should ensure that money transfer services are subject to the anti-money laundering legislation which applies to official banks. Furthermore, the FATF recommends that jurisdictions should designate an authority to grant licenses and ensure compliance.

Several jurisdictions already regulate money transfer agencies and services. In 1994, Italy extended the 1993 Bank Law against money laundering to financial intermediaries, including money transfer agencies. In the Netherlands, the Act on Money Transaction Offices (MTO Act) came into effect in 2002. The implementation of this Act meant that a wide range of money transaction offices were placed under the supervision of the Central Bank of the Netherlands, including money exchange offices, informal 'underground bankers' and non-banking money transfer agencies. According to this Act, money transaction offices have to be registered in order to function as licit offices. In the MTO Act, offices are obliged to pass on all information the competent authority deems necessary in order to ensure the proper execution of its duties.

In 1998, the Netherlands placed money transfer services under the Disclosure Act which means that 'unusual' money transfer transactions have to be reported to a Financial Intelligence Unit. Very recently the Dutch administration decided to widen the range of the Identification Services Act, so that financial institutes are obliged to identify the users of money transfers and to register and store the information for a period of five years.[56]

In 1998, Finland implemented an act in which various elements (disclosure, identification, registration) were consolidated in a single act, the Preventing and Clearing Money Laundering Act. The act also applies to non-banking institutions, such as money transfer offices. An important element of the act is the 'know your customer' principle. The service provider is obliged to obtain sufficient information concerning a customer's background or business and identity. Customer identification data must be stored for at least five years.[57]

Finland's report puts things in perspective. In Finland, numerous ideas have been considered, but fairly little has actually been done in the field of preventing economic crime and the use of companies in criminal activities. An explanation for this may be the business community's critical attitude to the idea of establishing control structures and practices to ensure the legality of business activities. The Finnish situation is important as it reveals the discrepancies between 'law in theory' and 'law in practice'. The effectiveness of legislation does not only depend on its presence, but also on the existence of a positive attitude to compliance with the rules and the possibilities of enforcement.

In principle, two control strategies can be applied to money transfers. The first strategy simply involves a partial or full prohibition of money transfers by non-banking institutions. The most decisive argument for this is that money transfers offer convenient opportunities for criminal use, without the possibility of effective regulation and supervision. The second strategy concerns licensing the use of money transfers. The most decisive argument against licensing is that prohibition would unduly harm the interests of legitimate users and it would seem unreasonable that these users should suffer from the deeds of illegitimate users. A choice has to be made between prohibition or regulation and the latter option seems to be preferable. However, opting for regulation has its drawbacks. A regulatory system which is not backed up by adequate administrative control, might lead to serious problems.

5.2 Informal Money or Value Transfer Systems

In many instances, other terms exist for informal money or value transfer systems: hawala, hundi, chiti banking, underground banking. 'Underground banking' is by far the most prevalent. However, it would be inaccurate to emphasise the secret ('underground') character of these 'banks', as in many countries they operate quite openly. The central issue is that money is transferred outside institutional financial channels which are supervised and monitored by the competent authorities (Passas, 1999: 10). 'Informal' is a fitting adjective for describing these activities, so we will use the term informal money or value transfer system (IMVTS).

56   Act on the Identification of Financial Services (*Wet Identificatie Financiële Dienstverlening*), 16 December
     1993, the Netherlands Statute book (*Stbl.*) 1993, 704, last amended by the Act of 2 November 2000, the
     Netherlands Statute book *(Stbl.)* 2000, 484
57   http://www.rata.bof.fi/english/Faq/data/data_money_laundering.html.

Just like money transfers, IMVTS is a system in which money (or value) is received for the purpose of paying it to a third party in another geographical location. Such transfers generally take place outside the conventional banking system through non-banking financial institutions or other business entities whose primary business activity may not be the transmission of money or value. This is the primary difference with money transfer organisations which have a formal and possibly licensed status as a money transfer agency.

To transfer money through an IMVTS, customers present funds to an IMVT operator and requests that they be transferred to a person at another location. The IMVT then communicates with an IMVT operator at the transfer destination requesting that funds be paid out to an individual identified by the initial customer. The communication may occur by telephone, facsimile or internet. The initial operator charges the customer a fee or percentage of the transfer amount. While in theory IMVT operations would tend to be balanced by funds being transferred in both directions, in practice the volume of transfers may be higher in one direction than another. The operators consequently need to settle their accounts, simply by using conventional banking systems, physical transfers or through a series of trade transactions (Kleemans *et al.*, 2002: 120).

In developed countries, IMVT systems are useful for immigrant populations wanting to repatriate earnings. The parties concerned are not subject to formal obligations in transferring money through an IMVT system. In theory, the senders and recipients are not obliged to provide identification. IMVT systems offer a quick and easy means of transferring money all over the world. The more that regulations restrict trade, currency exchange, or the movement of money through banking channels, the wider the use of IMVT is likely to be.

The most critical element in this informal system is the presence of trust. Without mutual trust between operators and clients, IMVT cannot operate. This is why strong social ties usually structure the network of IMVT operators and guarantee reliable and workable relationships. Their dependence on trust can even be considered to be a strength. In economic terms, the presence of trust makes IMVT relatively cheap, as it reduces transaction costs. For certain categories of customers, IMVT systems are therefore a more attractive means of transferring money than money transfers. Customers do not necessarily have criminal intentions. Linking IMVT exclusively or principally with crime does not correspond with the facts in many countries (Passas, 1999: 23).

Nevertheless, IMVT systems are attractive for transferring the proceeds of crime. The risks of detection and apprehension are very small. In theory, individual money transfers through IMVTS do not leave paper trails. Operators settle their accounts by adding up individual money transfers. Moreover, IMVT systems operate completely outside the scope of conventional financial monitoring systems. In practice, however, some IMVT operators appear to employ different working methods. The Dutch Organised Crime Monitor (Kleemans *et al.*, 1998 and 2002) provides us with a number of case studies which present a different picture of the methodology of some IMVT operators. The most important conclusion of this survey is that the informality of the system and the absence of paper trails appear to be well-preserved myths. Many IMVT operators do require their customers to provide identification and this information is even faxed to one another. They keep records of all their transactions and occasionally they use the services of official banks to transfer money (Kleemans *et al.*, 2002: 123-124). This implies that the possibility of detecting the use and misuse of these systems is more extensive than is often assumed.

5.2.1 Misuse of IMVT systems

Passas suggests that the growth of IMVT for hard-core criminal purposes is limited by the wide availability of numerous other alternatives and the incapacity of informal networks to handle very large sums of money on a regular basis. In his view "there is little evidence that the most sophisticated and organised criminals make use of IMVT" (Passas, 1999: 68).

In the Italian case studies, considerable information is available on the use of money transfers. Several cases demonstrate the use of intermediate agencies (i.e. Western Union Money Transfer); not one of the cases contains data about underground banking. Finland's national report mentions only one case in which underground banking "could have been used". The case pertains to heroin smuggling from India to Finland; the report postulates that the authorities' knowledge about Asian groups is generally very inadequate. In the Hungarian report, there are no references at all to IMVTS. The paucity of incidents would seem to confirm Passas' thesis.

It is interesting that the Dutch report contains more information about IMVTS. In a case concerning the smuggling of illegal immigrants through an underground banker, money was transferred from Western Europe to India; in another case an extended Iranian family was involved in underground banking. In addition, several case studies in the Dutch Organised Crime Monitor (Kleemans *et al.*, 2002) refer to IMVTS. Surprisingly, these cases contradict Passas' conclusions about the incapacity of IMVTS to handle very large sums of money. In one case a Turkish underground banker transferred 5 million euros (the proceeds of drug trafficking) from the Netherlands to Turkey. In another case, a Pakistani IMVTS managed to transfer 450,000 pounds sterling.

It is apparent that some IMVTS are indeed capable of processing large amounts of money. This finding is supported by the results of an English investigation which revealed that a Pakistan underground banker transferred 12 million pounds (just over 18 million euros) within a period of merely 6 months (Schaap, 2000: 107). Case studies mentioned in a recent FATF report also demonstrate the capability of some IMVT groups to transfer large sums of money (FATF, 2003).

5.2.2 Counter measures

Should IMVT be dealt with in exactly the same way as other remittance systems, i.e., that they should be subject to licensing and/or registration, and the same summary procedures as conventional financial institutions? In some jurisdictions this question has been answered positively. The Dutch MTO Act (2002) contains a wide definition of money transfers, including underground banking transactions. The act prescribes the criteria with which money transaction offices have to comply in order to be granted permission to execute financial transactions. Some jurisdictions have simply established licensing or registration systems; others do not have any specific arrangements for the regulation of IMVT (Passas, 1999). While the need to increase the transparency of such systems is becoming almost universally acknowledged, there is some concern that under certain circumstances an overly restrictive approach may have the opposite effect in pushing IMVT systems further underground (FATF, 2003: 10). This concern has been voiced by Passas. In his opinion, IMVT is the only available means for ethnic groups or minorities to send funds to their relatives in their countries of origin. These methods may also be used by illegal immigrants who have "perfectly legitimate jobs" (Passas, 1999: 68). He states that aggressive action against IMVT may be counterproductive, as it may drive a large number of generally law-abiding people to more radical solutions or criminal networks (Passas, *ibid.*). These adverse effects evidently have to be prevented. It is clear that solutions for dealing with IMVT systems must be found in the larger context of improving the infrastructure of basic financial services, primarily in the countries receiving IMVT transactions. Under these circumstances, advocating a less restrictive approach would not make sense. Due to the improved supervision of the banking sector, criminals are bound to revert to the opportunities provided by IMVT. The urgent need to prevent the criminal use of IMVT is thus greater than ever before. The introduction of money transfers has rendered the protection of the informal status of IMVT obsolete. Money transfers meet the needs of ethnical groups for easy and fast global money transfers. The adverse effects caused by regulation which Passas fears, do not necessarily have to take place. It is more likely that the current legitimate users of IMVT will opt for money transfer systems instead.

5.3 Conclusion and recommendations

Money transfer and IMVT systems are important financial services. They are fast and safe. From the perspective of the offender they are safe in the sense that they leave relatively little evidence and that – up until now – transactions can be executed without the need for any official identification documents. In the last few years, the safety aspect has been 'under pressure'. In a special recommendation, the FATF proposed that information about the sending party is immediately made available to the police and prosecuting authorities. These non-banking institutions are increasingly being placed under the ambit of anti-money laundering regulations, which already exist for the banking sector (Levi, 2002). Basically, strengthening supervision and control could have two divergent effects. On the one hand, it could provoke non-banks – in particular IMVT agencies – to go further underground. On the other hand, it might result in a situation in which the use of IMVT will no longer be advantageous in comparison with money transfers.

6 Forged official documents

Jurjen Boorsma[58]

Forged documents are important for the smooth operation of criminal activities. Forged Bills of Loading help to safely conceal drugs in containers. Smuggling illegal immigrants is immensely facilitated by the use forged identity documents. In this chapter we will direct our attention to the forgery of *identity* (or *travel*) documents, as there has been a significant increase in the trade and possession of these documents during the last fifteen years. The demand for high quality forged documents is constantly on the increase. This increase is due to a number of factors.

Firstly, the influx of illegal immigrants into Europe is important. Since the fall of the Berlin Wall, this influx does not just consist of people originating from third world countries, but it also includes East Europeans. Even though the European Commission refuses to calculate an estimate,[59] millions of illegal immigrants currently reside in the European Union. Secondly, within the framework of prevention policy and in order to bar illegal immigrants as well as fight organised crime, the scope of identification and checking the residence status have been expanded throughout all segments of society. In other words, the increase of preventive measures has resulted in an increase in the need for false documents. This chapter will focus on the instruments available to diminish the number of high quality forged identity documents. We will discuss the technical possibilities available to tackle forgery and argue that in addition to technical instruments, the effectiveness of this approach depends on human input.

6.1 Risk factors and key problems

One of the most striking 'red flags' we encountered in our analyses of the national reports, is the importance of false travel documents. The Italian cases display the frequent use of false identity documents. It was concluded that propulsive and facilitating contacts among criminal groups exist in the area of stolen and counterfeited documents. Another 'red flag' identified by the Italians is the format and regulation of identity documents. Some of the Italian case studies demonstrate that the security levels of identity documents need to be greatly increased. The report recommends more effective checks on the authenticity of identity documents using, for instance, electronic surveillance systems and making documents more foolproof.

The Hungarian report similarly concludes that new types of personal documents should be introduced to make the work of forgers considerably more difficult. The Finnish report states: "To confuse the law enforcement authorities, organised

---

58 Jurjen Boorsma, L.L.M., is a criminologist and works as a financial detective for the National Criminal Investigations of the National Police Corps.

59 Question E-3547/01 by Erik Meijer (GUE/NGL) written to the Commission, Rise in crime due to the increase in the proportion of the urban population of no known name, nationality, address or source of income, *OJ C 301 E*, 05/12/2002, pp. 12-13.

crime groups in Russia and Estonia provide their employees *(victims of women trafficking)* with easily available false travelling documents and often with several different identities too. The problem is being countered by checking the fingerprints of those suspected of using multiple identities." The use of forged documents has been detected in the Dutch cases as well. All cases relate to women trafficking for the purpose of their exploitation in Dutch brothels. In particular, the Italian and Hungarian cases demonstrate how 'identity fraud' is related to the smuggling of illegal immigrants conducted by Chinese criminal organisations and women trafficking by Albanian organisations. Three Italian cases are connected to Chinese Triads and five cases are connected to Albanian groups. In the small-scale Hungarian cases, it is striking that of the 180 people who were smuggled, 51 of them originated from China and 54 from Albania.

It is impossible to estimate the number of false documents in circulation. Nevertheless, some sources indicate that the number is very large indeed. In the Netherlands, a nation with a population of sixteen million people, 435,000 Dutch passports were reported missing or stolen in the period 1996-2000. [60] In the year 2001, 2,934 individuals were prosecuted for the use of false documents and 146 individuals were prosecuted for the fabrication of false passports. [61] Notwithstanding the lack clarity regarding the seriousness of the problem, society's interest in proper identity checks is increasing. Despite the fact that we have open borders, border checks are still an important instrument. Inhabitants from over 130 countries are required to be in possession of a so-called 'Schengen visa' if they wish to be admitted to a country within the Schengen zone. Illegal immigrants who wish to settle and work in Europe have become aware of the fact that they always need an identity document with a valid status of residence. Moreover, illegal immigrants are faced with an additional problem: Europe and a number of other countries have introduced a personal identification number. Generally, only legal inhabitants or aliens with a working permit are eligible for receiving this number.

6.2 Existing measures

Over the last few decades, the vulnerability of passports to fraud has decreased immensely. Since the 1960s, the number and complexity of authenticity marks on passports have been increased, such as the use of hallmarked paper, extra layers of laminate, intricate methods of binding and measures against soaking off pictures. [62] Nevertheless, analyses of critical studies and several case studies

60 Abuse and improper use in the area of tax, social security and subsidies (*Misbruik en oneigenlijk gebruik op het gebied van belastingen, sociale zekerheid en subsidies*), letter from the Minister of Justice, *Kamerstukken II* 2001/02, 17 050; p. 33.
61 Abuse and improper use in the area of tax, social security and subsidies (*Misbruik en oneigenlijk gebruik op het gebied van belastingen, sociale zekerheid en subsidies*), letter from the Minister of Justice, *Kamerstukken II* 2001/02, 17 050; p. 34.

indicate that these preventive measures have had only limited effects. Technical improvements have resulted in improved forgeries: even hallmarked paper or extra layers of laminate can be imitated. However, there are a number of existing measures which help to tackle forgery and fraud related to identity documents. Firstly, the safe storage of blank passports is an important countermeasure against theft. In the Netherlands, the personal information in passports used to be printed out by city councils. In the 1990s, however, town halls with inadequate security were subject to burglaries and passports were amongst the stolen goods. Since then, Dutch passports have no longer been fabricated in town halls, but in a central and well-secured location. It should be noted that passports are still being stolen from European consulates. Secondly, several countries now link their databases. For instance, governments are able to prevent people from obtaining official identity documents under the name of a deceased person, if the application for a passport and the population register are linked or if these government services are run by the same organisation.[63] Checking the social security number can reveal identity fraud and it also has a preventive effect. Thirdly, the Belgian police have been checking the presence of false documents in airmail and on packages carried by couriers. Despite the fact these checks were carried out by only four officials, the taskforce confiscated a total of 875 courier packages and 340 postal deliveries in 1999. More then twenty percent of the 362 units of airmail coming from Albania contained false passports (CGKR, 2000).[64] Finally, inspectors have to be aware of the specific items on a passport that identify or reveal forgeries. False identity documents from distant non-European countries, e.g. an Asian birth certificate, can be used to obtain a valid identity document in a European country. Needless to say, in relation to this sort of document inspectors are not always able to distinguish counterfeit documents from original ones. In order to tackle this type of fraud, several European countries have established a computer database entitled the Edison Document System. This database contains the hallmarks of over 1,500 travel documents from all over the world.

6.3 Possible preventive measures and best practices

6.3.1 Technological improvements

The possibilities for prevention basically consist of an extension of the existing measures: the continuing development of the technical enhancement of identity documents, the further improvement of the security in storing and distributing identity documents, the large-scale linking of databases and extending the accessibility to information about hallmarks, the installation of biometrics, the

---

62 An overview of improvements in English identity documents can be found at http://www.ukpa.gov.uk/_history.
63 'Immigration Crime Team Targets Identity Hijackers Across U.K., press release ICT/National Crime Squad, http://www.ukpa.gov.uk/downloads/ICT2.pdf.
64 The CGKR is the Belgian Centre for Equal Opportunities and Opposition to Racism (*Centrum voor gelijkheid van kansen en voor racismebestrijding*), data can be found at http://www.antiracisme.be.

education of counter clerks and the availability of the serial numbers of missing passports. These are all measures which would reinforce those already existing. The European Commission has recently introduced a programme concerning external borders, visas, asylum and immigration in which biometric identifiers are applied for the identification of persons.[65]

Prevention policy should subsequently aim at minimizing the wide range of possibilities that forgers have at their disposal. Almost two hundred countries throughout the world distribute over ten thousand different identity papers, such as visas, birth certificates and driver's licenses. Forgers can simply choose the documents which are easiest to copy or forge. This demonstrates how much the global community could benefit from national and international standardisation. Even though global standardisation would not be feasible, a continuation of European standardisation is certainly achievable. On a national level, a potential for improvements can also be detected; some registration procedures still allow the use of *copies* of passports. This type of registration is evidently highly sensitive to fraud.

Source documents, e.g. application forms, birth and marriage certificates and copies of the population register, can be equipped with hallmarks. Source documents distributed in high-risk countries should be verified by the embassies in the countries of origin. The prevention policies of embassies and consulates requires constant attention. Diplomatic support points are also the outposts of Europe. At the same time, it is important to set up expertise centres in Western countries that will disseminate knowledge on the verification of documents. The Belgian 'best practice' of checking international postal deliveries to high-risk countries has proven to be most effective. This policy should spread to other countries. However, even though the results might prove worthwhile, investigating authorities often lack the capacity to track the forger and addressee; the absence of highly qualified forgers would seriously damage the logistic process of criminal organisations.

6.3.2 Human work

The detection of false documents does not solely depend on the abovementioned technical instruments. The efforts of inspectors are of vital importance as well; the better they do their work, the more forged documents will be identified. Organisations which are easily deceived by low-quality forgeries undermine the effectiveness of the technical security of identity documents. The swift detection of false documents is the only way to effectively discourage forgery. Governments need to ensure that the entire chain of people and entities involved are effective in checking identity. However, not everyone is easily committed; commercial parties often consider that the extra workload and the anticipated increase in bureaucracy will clash with their commercial interests or their customers' rights to privacy.

65   Annual work programme and call for proposals 2003 (ARGO), *OJ C 111*, 09/05/2003, p. 5.

Dutch agencies and organisations cooperate under a platform entitled
Initiatiefgroep Identiteitsvaststelling. This platform enables banks, social security
agencies, the police and department of justice, the aliens and naturalisation
office and the population registration service to communicate with one another.
Their shared innovations, education and exchange of knowledge is realised
through the platform. The participants have organised a common education
programme which teaches people how to recognise false documents. A research
programme has also been initiated that examines the possibilities of gearing
computer systems to one another. In addition, this research programme
investigates potential improvements in the cooperation between agencies which
are responsible for the registration of aliens (e.g. the concentration of services
and use of one computer system).[66] This resulted in the establishment of the
'National Bureau of Documents' in June 2003 which shares concrete information
on forgeries, encourages the development of methods of inspection and offers
training courses for inspectors.

The continuing debate about the necessity of effective checks on documents is
vital to its success. Investigations at the addresses of employers suggest that in
some cases of identity fraud, employers had consciously been negligent or had
even supported the fraud; employment agencies and companies had used illegal
immigrants with false social registration numbers to do heavy-duty and irregular
work, without asking them for a passport (Dekker, 2002).

Another example of the importance of debate is the reluctance of airline
companies to conform to their legal obligation to adequately check their
passengers' identity documents (pre-flight checks). As a consequence, these
companies facilitate illegal immigrants entering the country by air. A criminal
complaint lodged by the Dutch government forced a Dutch company to
conform to the law.[67] Several years ago, German and British airline companies
were involved in similar court procedures.

6.4   Conclusions and recommendations

There is a wide availability of technical instruments for the protection of identity
documents against forgery and the verification of people's identity. Though
important for its success, prevention involves more than just the use of technical
instruments such as linked databases, safe storage facilities, stricter application
and distribution procedures, accessible information on hallmarks, thorough
check-ups of foreign source documents and a continuous strive for
standardisation.

Ultimately, the most crucial element in successful and effective prevention is
the commitment of the people who are in charge of checking documents.

66   BIZZO publications, '*Grotere pakkans bij fraude met identiteiten*' http://www.bizzo.nl/PUBLICATIES/
ARTIKELEN/pakkans.html.
67   For the jurisdiction see Supreme Court (HR) 11 June 2000, *NJ* 2002, 373, No.112.986.

When checks fail, it is not just a matter of negligence. If employers do not have a commercial interest in checking their employees and airline companies refuse to perform sound boarding checks for the same reasons, preventive measures are of no use whatsoever.

Moreover, forged documents pose a fundamental threat to all preventive strategies. Whether it concerns financial transactions, trade in weapons and explosives, the licit or illicit purchase of large amounts of raw materials for synthetic drugs or the establishment of legal persons, the essential question is always: who is the customer? The proper checking of identity is the door to the success of other preventive measures in the framework of organised crime. If the foundation does not hold, the fortress will fall.

7 Conclusions and recommendations

Henk van de Bunt and Cathelijne van der Schoot [68]

Within the framework of the European Community, preventive action against organised crime has been launched on many fronts. Several *individual* measures aimed at the prevention of certain organised crime activities have come into force since the early 1990s, e.g. the anti-money laundering measures to prevent the abuse of the financial system. The first signs of the European Union's *structural* needs for the prevention of organised crime date back to 1996, when the Stockholm conference examined the prevention of crime connected with European economic integration and social exclusion. The Treaty of Amsterdam then included the importance of the prevention of crime (organised or not) in policies of the European Union for the creation of an area of freedom, security and justice. [69] The *Action Plan to Combat Organized Crime* adopted by the European Council on 28 April 1997 summed up a large number of recommendations to make the preventive approach more specific. Some recommendations pertain to reducing the demand for illegal products and services, e.g. by destroying the breeding ground for organised crime (improving the labour market). Several other recommendations refer to the increase in the defensibility of the licit environment (anti-corruption policy) and other proposals concern the decrease in opportunities (protection of personal, pivotal information).

The innovative aspect of this preventive approach is the fact that it is not primarily aimed at the perpetrators of organised crime, but rather at the facilitating circumstances of organised crime. The preventive approach addresses governments, civilians and enterprises and it tries to make them feel responsible for the prevention of organised crime. Appealing for an integrated approach introduces another important innovation; combating organised crime is no longer the exclusive responsibility of criminal justice agencies. The 60 case studies in the national reports and the last four chapters of this report provide us with essential insights into organised crime, the interaction between law enforcement agencies and interfaces with legitimate sectors in society. [70] A clear picture of the possibilities that – intentionally or not – are offered by the legitimate world has thus been created. We have been forced to recognize that organised crime is facilitated by the existence of a demand for illegal products and services. Furthermore, we have recognised the low-level accessibility of licit services. A distinction has been made between the facilitators of the licit environment (facilitators with technical or legal know-how which

---

68   Henk van de Bunt is Professor in Criminology at Erasmus University Rotterdam and the Vrije Universiteit Amsterdam, and Cathelijne van der Schoot is PhD candidate at the Department of Criminology at Erasmus University Rotterdam.

69   This aspect was again emphasised at the European Council of Tampere in 1999. Presidency conclusions, Tampere, European Council of 15-16 October 1999, points 41-42 of the conclusion.

70   Although files from closed police investigations of criminal groups provide access to unique, reliable and valid data, it must be pointed out that this method is time-consuming and in many countries there is no tradition of such empirical research into organised crime.

enables criminal organisations to operate financial transactions, such as public officials and legal persons) and the availability of tools in the licit environment (false documents, legal persons, raw materials for synthetic drugs and firearms). Chapter 2 sketches the preventive measures which have been proposed by the four participating countries.

These findings offer many clues for situational prevention and the prevention of victimisation. The underlying message is actually quite simple: if criminal organisations are able to easily acquire or access resources, then the number of these resources has to be reduced, or made more difficult to acquire or access. In other words: the observation that false documents provide easy access to countries (relevant in the case of human smuggling) or the services of financial institutions, should result in a decrease of the number of false documents in circulation (by making them foolproof; by prioritising the prosecution of forgers) and improved security in the storage of documents (placing blank passports in safes in town halls) and improved validity checks by custom officials and other controllers. It appears that many preventive measures aim to restrict the presence of accessibility to resources for criminal associations. Appendix 2 and 3 give brief summaries of, respectively, all the opportunities which were detected and the preventive measures which were presented.

In addition to these rather specific conditions, the national reports and the previous four chapters elaborated on more general conditions such as unambiguous legislation and the exchange of information which would have to be carried out in order to give preventive measures an effective impact. Although expressed in different terms, all the authors adhere to the same message: *prevention is not self-executing.* Successful prevention requires an active attitude and not a passive one: it will not happen of its own accord. It requires awareness or even perhaps a sense of urgency on behalf of the people in charge. Chapter 6, which focused on forged official documents, explains that no matter how good and sophisticated the security relating to documents may be, it is the human factor which remains the weakest link.

In this last chapter we will consider the question concerning the conditions which have to be fulfilled in order to carry out prevention. Firstly, we will discuss awareness (7.1). Secondly, we will focus on two other relevant conditions, which can be summarised as 'ensuring the provision of sound information facilities' (7.2) and 'an unambiguous attitude in enforcement' (7.3).

7.1   Awareness

Let us commence with a concrete example taken from the Finnish national report. The report points out that immigrants who receive welfare service flats are usually unaware of the existance of the rules which stipulate the conditions under which a third party can or cannot be accommodated. Simply increasing the information concerning these restrictions and the related sanctions would keep a decent number of potential facilitators out of the criminal market.

The social welfare authorities could supervise the actual use of welfare service accommodation more effectively as well, when renting or buying real estate. In short, a small increase in awareness could restrict a decent number of potential facilitators from storerooms and remove a considerable facilitating factor for drug trafficking and human trafficking.

The measures and best practices mentioned in the previous chapters, demonstrate that, fortunately, there is an increase in the cooperation between public and private organisations, in order to inform and notify each other about the risks of organised crime. The project 'Security Main port Rotterdam', for instance, provides agencies and large companies who are active in Rotterdam harbour with specified and specific crime risks, concrete examples of crime and a guide which contains many concrete recommendations, in order to prevent the harbour falling victim to criminal penetration (see Chapter 3).

Awareness should involve more than just having 'knowledge about something'. It is important that people have the courage to act accordingly. Financial organisations who are aware of illegal transactions should not be deterred from disclosing information about such transactions due to the fear of legal claims on the part of their clients. Drivers who refuse to transport suspicious cargo should be protected from customers as well as their employers; informers and witnesses in criminal cases should be able to speak up and testify without being confronted with damaging repercussions. It is therefore of great importance to adopt legislation and concrete facilities which help people who dare to act and speak out under difficult circumstances. In some countries, governments protect their financial organisations by safeguarding them against customers whose transactions have been disclosed without proper reasons; in the last few years, the legal position of informers and employees who refuse illegal services has been improved.

Awareness is not something which can be taken for granted. The parties involved have to recognise the importance of being aware. Up until recently, professionals and businessmen could use their ignorance of the criminal use of their services as a justification. They would claim naivety as an excuse or that they did not perceive it as their responsibility to verify the purpose behind their clients' requests. Thanks to new legislation and government policy this attitude is changing. Nowadays service providers can be held responsible (under civil or criminal law) if they conduct transactions with criminal customers without properly investigating their clients. A good example is the criminal case that the Dutch government initiated against KLM (Royal Dutch Airlines) where KLM failed to comply with their legal obligation to conduct sound pre-boarding flight checks, which resulted in them facilitating human smuggling. KLM was convicted and the company is currently more aware of the fact that airline companies can be subject to abuse for criminal purposes.

The government and, in particular, administrative agencies (the internal revenue service and social welfare) need to increase their awareness. Before the 'discovery' of money laundering in the early 1990s, tax inspectors primarily focused on tax declarations which were too low. The assumption was that civilians wished to pay as little tax as possible. The 'mind-shift' came in the mid-1990s, when the authorities realised that criminals were trying to inflate their turnover and profits as much as possible in order to legitimise the proceeds of crime.

Customs also have a greater sense of awareness, which has led to a different checking method. Up until recently, their main task was checking incoming goods and persons. Today, in the scope of countering organised crime, greater attention is paid to outgoing traffic. The Dutch blind spot in relation to outgoing traffic is symbolised by its legislation: it penalises the smuggling of illegal immigrants *to* the Netherlands, but it fails to penalise the smuggling of illegal immigrants *from* the Netherlands.

The essence of the prevention of organised crime is basically reducing the opportunities which enable crime to take place and criminal proceeds to be processed. In terms of improved supervision – leading to a reduction of opportunities – an important task lies ahead for public administration as a whole, for it has a vital supervisory function (regulation of financial institutions; border checks; alien checks).

This task cannot be performed properly without awareness. It plays a pivotal role. This requires public agencies to be well aware of their own vulnerabilities. Awareness presupposes good governance and at the very least, the integrity of its agencies. The prevention of organised crime entails a constructive attitude in the working of an organisation, meaning the creation of more transparency in the decision-making process, the consolidation of procedures and the instruction of personnel. Such remarks concerning awareness presuppose that the private and public parties which are involved are in themselves *bona fide*. Should this not be the case – e.g. when organised crime has deeply penetrated legitimate parts of society – the situational approach would be totally ineffective.

7.2 Being well-informed

Prevention is a matter of thinking and acting in advance. In this respect it can be distinguished from criminal repressive action. Prevention is pro-active, criminal measures are naturally reactive. Prevention enables intervention to take place before the injustice has been fully realised. There is always a risk of the incarceration of innocent people (those who are within the range of the intervention) or the escape of those who should be incarcerated.

An effective preventive approach requires decision makers to be well informed. They need to be sufficiently knowledgeable about organised crime in general, as well as possess specific knowledge concerning individual cases. This applies to governments as well as civilians or companies who are undertaking tasks in the field of prevention. An appropriate saying could be: 'Know your customer'.

When it comes to 'knowing your customer', identity documents play a vital role, e.g. financial services sometimes require customers to identify themselves. False documents destroy the effectiveness of this preventive strategy. They can seriously mislead the people checking the documents and service providers. It is therefore important to invest in reducing opportunities for document forgery. Chapter 6 provides a number of concrete examples which demonstrate how the verification of documents can be improved and which techniques can be applied in order to reduce the susceptibility to identity fraud. This does not only involve the identities of natural persons, but also those of legal persons. The national reports demonstrate that Italy, Finland and the Netherlands have created databanks which contain information about legal persons. These databanks allow the authorities to identify a person who, as a founder or board member, is using a legal person as a cover.

Italy and the Netherlands have implemented legislation that allows the administrative agencies to refuse permits or the commission of projects to companies who are suspected of being involved in organised crime. These suspicions must be backed up with reliable evidence, verifiable by the applicant, and in the case of Italy, also by court. This is naturally not problematic if a criminal conviction has taken place. However, in many cases a criminal conviction has not taken place and the only source available is confidential police information. For this reason, it would be desirable to set up an agency which has legal status and the authorisation to check applications for permits, tender proposals etc. on the basis of all types of databases, and with the authorisation to force companies to cooperate with the agency's investigations. Furthermore, a recommendation would be to amend the verification framework for granting and withdrawing permits, in a whole range of legislation (Fijnaut 2002). As was pointed out in Chapter 4, Italy and The Netherlands have already taken such measures.

An integral and preventive approach towards crime will sooner or later encounter problems in the exchange of information between the participants. Each agency has its own competence in the collection of information. This affects cooperation, particularly that between services with completely different backgrounds, e.g. judicial and administrative agencies. The inadequacies in the information sharing system will cause a backlog in the government's knowledge about criminal associations. It is important to implement comprehensive legislation to govern the exchange of information and the status of databanks (which are managed by several agencies).

Finally, it is important to systematically gather information on the phenomenon of organised crime itself. Police investigation files provide an important source of information. Following the Dutch Organised Crime Monitor, this research contains the analyses and description of concrete case studies. The possibilities of using police files for different types of analysis are diverse. In this respect, Hungary has rather a low score in comparison with Finland, Italy and the Netherlands. The adoption by other countries of the Dutch system of the Organised Crime Monitor is recommended. These particular case studies do not only encourage knowledge-based prevention and the adoption of preventive measures, but their use in drawing up systematic international comparisons may lead to enhanced insight into the similarities and differences regarding organised crime in the Member States of the European Union. Moreover, information regarding the abuse of facilitators or the availability of logistic facilities could also be revealed in police investigations. By using the 'Twin-Track' approach, police investigations could combine a problem-oriented policy towards criminal activities with the detection of crime-facilitating opportunities for the purposes of situational prevention, as described by the Commission of the European Communities (SEC (2001) 433).

7.3   Striving for consistency

The national reports indicate that the attitudes of governments and businesses towards organised crime are often ambiguous. It is important to recognise how the existence of organised crime is beneficial to some institutions and that some institutions are not interested in the fight against organised crime. It is impossible to estimate the full effect that preventive actions have. It is therefore important that preventive action is always carefully assessed taking other existing interests into consideration. For example, a balance would have to be achieved between checking harbour imports and exports and the economic interests of the rapid circulation of goods. An important issue is whether the course of justice has been subordinated to these economical interests or not. For instance, the Dutch report observes that the possibilities of smuggling goods across the Dutch borders are so extensive, that crime syndicates have virtually no need to corrupt custom officials. The importance of economic interests would be reduced if the European Union would homogenise their standards of checks and supervision. Unfair competition arises when countries apply different rules and policies for checks, e.g. regarding main harbours.

The re-calibration of economical interests is not the only issue at hand. Chapter 5 stresses the position of lawyers and the principle of confidentiality between lawyers and their clients. This principle practically masks everything which occurs within the scope of this relationship. Should the legal professions maintain their exceptional position, or should they reveal any information on unusual transactions and thus be subjected to the same set of rules which apply for financial institutions? Is the right of non-disclosure absolute, or is it time to reconsider the scope of this principle? It is conceivable that the scope of this legally stipulated right is restricted to the interactions between lawyer and client which concern support in the legal process.

In short, if governments attach great importance to the prevention of organised crime, this has to be reflected when clear and distinct choices are made in considering the different interests involved. Moreover, governments have to be unambiguous in their legalisation or the prohibition of certain activities, such as the exploitation of brothels or underground banks. Preventive policy, namely the administrative prevention of organised crime is only effective in regulating legal markets. When criminal activities are conducted in illegal markets, administrative measures will not be directed towards the principal criminal activities. This implies that by legalising certain activities related to organised crime, the opportunity will be created to use administrative instruments to fight organised crime. Exchange bureaus, underground banks and brothels therefore need to be taken out of the twilight zone of pseudo-illicitness (formal prohibition, but in practice condoning illegal activities). The legalisation of brothels, for example, will provide the administrative government with the possibility of separating brothels from the criminal environment by being able to research the permits and antecedents of brothel owners.

To conclude, in order to prevent organised crime from subjecting the opportunities provided by the licit environment to abuse, it is of vital importance that governments, businesses and legal professions properly conduct their tasks of supervision and checks. They basically function as the gatekeepers of the licit world; they have the power to prevent organised crime from accessing the facilities of the licit world. In this context, they play a key role in the preservation of the integrity of society and the prevention of the further infiltration of organised crime. A strong gatekeeper is aware, well-informed and unafraid to makes choices.

References

Legislation

The abuse and improper use in the areas of tax, social security and subsidies (*Misbruik en oneigenlijk gebruik op het gebied van belastingen, sociale zekerheid en subsidies*), Letter from the Minister of Justice, *Kamerstukken II* 2001/02, 17 050

Act on the Identification of Financial Services (*Wet Identificatie Financiële Dienstverlening*), 16 December 1993, the Netherlands Statute book (*Stbl.*) 1993, 704, last amended by the Act of 2 November 2000, *Stbl.* 2000, 484

Act on Money Transaction Offices *(Wet inzake de geldtransactiekantoren)*, 27 June 2002, *Stbl.* 2002, 380

Act amending Alien Act and several other acts in order to link aliens' rights towards administrative bodies regarding the provisions, facilities, benefits, exemptions and permits to the legal residence aliens in the Netherlands (*Koppelingswet*), 26 March 1998, *Stbl.* 1998, 203

Action Plan of 28 April 1997 to combat organised crime, *OJ C 251*, 15/08/1997, pp. 1-16

Annual work programme and call for proposals 2003 (ARGO), *OJ C 111*, 09/05/2003, pp. 2-8

Council Directive on the prevention of the use of the financial system for the purpose of money laundering of 10 June 1991, *OJ L 166*, 28/06/1991, pp. 77-83

Council Resolution of 21 December 1998 on the Prevention of Organized Crime with Reference to the Establishment of a Comprehensive Strategy for Combating it, *OJ C 408*, 29/12/98, pp. 1-4

Directive 2001/97/EC of the European Parliament and of the Council of 4 December 2001, amending Council Directive 91/308/EEC on the prevention of the use of the financial system for the purpose of money laundering, *OJ L 344*, 28/12/01, pp. 76-82

European Parliament and Council Directive 97/52/EC of 13 October 1997 amending directives 92/50/EEC, 93/36/EEC and 93/37/EEC concerning the coordination of procedures for awarding public service contracts, public supply contracts and public works contracts, *OJ L 328*, 28/11/1997, pp. 1-59

Joint Action plan of 19 March 1998 adopted by the Council, on the basis of Article K.3 of the Treaty on European Union, establishing a programme of exchanges, training and cooperation for persons responsible for action to combat organised crime (Falcone programme), *OJ L 099*, 31/03/1998, pp. 8-12

K4 Committee, 'Elaboration of a common mechanism for the collection and systematic analysis of information on international organised crime', *Enfopol 161*, rev. I, The Council of the European Union, Brussels, 1994

Policy regarding XTC (*Beleid inzake XTC*), *Handelingen II* 2000/01, 23 760, No. 14, pp. 10-11

Programme for police and judicial cooperation in criminal matters (Programme AGIS) – Annual work programme and call for applications for 2003, *OJ C 5.* 10/01/03, pp. 5-18

Proposal for a Council Decision establishing a programme of incentives and exchanges, training and cooperation for the prevention of crime (Hippocrates), *OJ C 096 E*, 27/03/2001, pp. 244-246

The prevention and control of organised crime: a European Union strategy for the beginning of the new millennium, *OJ C 124*, 03/05/2000, pp. 1-33

Towards a European strategy to prevent organised crime, Commission staff working paper, *SEC (2001) 433*

Treaty of Amsterdam amending the treaty on European Union, the treaties establishing the European Communities and related acts, *OJ C 340*, 10/11/1997

United Nations Convention Against Transnational Organised Crime, Italy, Palermo, December 2000, art. 3

Question E-3547/01 written by Erik Meijer (GUE/NGL) to the Commission, "Rise in crime due to the increase in the proportion of the urban population of no known name, nationality, address or source of income", *OJ C 301 E*, 05/12/2002, pp. 12-13

Bibliography

Albanese, J.S.
The Prediction and Control of Organized Crime. A Risk Assessment Instrument for Targeting Law Enforcement Efforts, 2001
Summary Report, S.1

Bennett, T.H.
'Crime prevention', in: Tonry, M. (ed.), *The Handbook of Crime and Punishment*
New York: Oxford University Press, 1998, pp. 369-402

Bovenkerk, F., M. Komen and Y. Yesilgöz (eds.)
Multiculturaliteit in de strafrechtspleging
The Hague: Boom, 2003

Brink, H., M. Brodie-Barendregt, A.B. Hoogenboom, A. van Galen and A. Roos
Criminaliteitsbeeld Rotterdamse haven
Rotterdam: Kernteam Rotterdam-Rijnmond, 2002

Bunt, H.G. van de, and E.R. Kleemans
'Transnational organized crime. New directions for empirical research and public policy', in: Bruinsma, G.J.N., Elffers, H. and J. de Keijser (eds.), *Punishment, Places, and Perpetrators: Developments in Criminology and Criminal Justice Research*
Devon: Willan Publishing, 2003 (forthcoming)

Centre for International Crime Prevention
'Assessing Transnational Organized Crime: Results of a Pilot Survey of 40 Selected Organized Criminal Groups in 16 Countries', *Trends in Organized Crime*, 6 (2), 2000, pp. 44-92

CGKR
Beeldvorming van de mensenhandel en analyse van de rechtspraak; Jaarverslag mensenhandel 2000
Brussels: Centrum voor gelijkheid van kansen en voor racismebestrijding, 2001

CGKR
Tussen beleid en middelen: de diepe kloof?; Jaarverslag mensenhandel 1999
Brussels: Centrum voor gelijkheid van kansen en voor racismebestrijding, 2000

Clarke, R.V.
Situational crime prevention: successful case studies
New York: Harrow and Heston, 1997

Cressey, D.R.
Theft of the Nation; the structure and operations of organised crime in America
New York: Harper & Row, 1969

Daalder, A.
Het bordeelverbod opgeheven
The Hague: WODC, 2002

Dekker, C.J.
Project Sofi-nummers 2000 – 2001, Onderzoek naar misbruik en oneigenlijk gebruik van Sofi-nummers
Amsterdam, UWV GAK, 2002

Della Porta, D. and A. Vannucci
Corrupt Exchanges. Actors, Resources, and Mechanisms of Political Corruption
New York: Aldine de Gruyter, 1999

Di Nicola, A. and C. Brentari
"Italy", in: White, S. (ed.), *Procurement and Organised Crime; an EU-wide Study*
London: Institute of Advanced Legal Studies, 2000

Dijk, J. van, and J. Waard
'A two-dimensial typology of crime prevention projects: with a bibliography',
Criminal Justice Abstracts, 23, pp. 483-503, 1991

Duyne, P.C. van *et al.*
Misdaadondernemingen; ondernemende misdadigers in Nederland
Deventer: Gouda Quint, 1990

Duyne, P.C.
Het spook en de dreiging van de georganiseerde criminaliteit
The Hague: Sdu, 1995

FATF (Financial Action Task Force on Money Laundering)
1998-1999 Report on money laundering typologies
Paris: FATF, 1999b

FATF (Financial Action Task Force on Money Laundering)
Annual report 1998-1999
Paris: FATF, 1999a

FATF (Financial Action Task Force on Money Laundering)
Annual report 1999
Paris: FATF, 2000

FATF (Financial Action Task Force on Money Laundering)
Report on money laundering typologies 2000-2001
Paris: FATF, 2001

FATF (Financial Action Task Force on Money Laundering)
Report on Money Laundering Typologies 2002-2003
Paris: FATF, 2003

FATF (Financial Action Task Force on Money Laundering)
Review of the FATF's Forty Recommendations; Consultation paper
Paris: FATF, 2002

Fijnaut, C.
'The administrative approach to organised crime in Amsterdam: backgrounds
and developments', in: Fijnaut, C. (ed.), *The administrative approach to
(organised) crime in Amsterdam*
Amsterdam: Public Order and Safety Department City of Amsterdam, 2002

Fijnaut, C., F. Bovenkerk, G. Bruinsma and H. van de Bunt
*Inzake opsporing: Bijlage VIII; Autochtone, allochtone en buitenlandse
criminele groepen*
Den Haag: Sdu, 1996, pp. 129-148 and pp. 179-186

Fijnaut, C., F. Bovenkerk, G. Bruinsma and H. van de Bunt
*Inzake opsporing: Bijlage X; De vrije beroepsbeoefenaars: advocaten, notarissen
en accountants*
Den Haag: Sdu, 1996, pp. 9-27

Fijnaut, C., F. Bovenkerk, G. Bruinsma and H. van de Bunt
Organized crime in the Netherlands
The Hague: Kluwer Law International, 1998

Garland, D.
'The limits of the sovereign sate; strategies of crime control in contemporary societies', *The British Journal of Criminology*, 36 (4), 1996, pp. 445-471

Graham, J. and T.H. Bennet
Crime prevention strategies in Europe en North America
Helsinki: Heuni, 1995

Heddeghem, K. van, T. van der Beken, G. Vermeulen and B. de Ruyver
Gewapend bestuursrecht gescreend
Antwerp: Maklu, 2002

Home Office Research Development and Statistics Directorate
NCIS, Swedish Crime Prevention Council, Europol, *The Identification, Development and Exchange of Good Practices for Reducing Organised Crime*, 2001 (draft version March 2001)

Jacobs, J., C. Friel and R. Radick
Gotham Unbound; How New York City was Liberated from the Grip of Organized Crime
New York: New York University Press, 1999

Kaiser, G.
Kriminologie; Ein Lehrbuch
Heidelberg: Mueller Juridischer Verlag, 1988

Kleemans, E., E. van den Berg and H. van de Bunt
Georganiseerde criminaliteit in Nederland; rapportage op basis van de WODC-monitor
The Hague: WODC, 1998

Kleemans, E., M. Brienen and H. van de Bunt
Georganiseerde criminaliteit in Nederland; rapportage op basis van de WODC-monitor
The Hague: WODC, 2002

Levi, M.
Terrorist Finance and Money Laundering: A new paradigm for crime control?
unpublished, 2002

Manunza, E.
EG-aanbestedingsrechtelijke problemen bij privatiseringen en bij de bestrijding van corruptie en georganiseerde criminaliteit
Deventer: Kluwer, 2001

Meldpunt Ongebruikelijke Transacties
Jaarverslag van het Meldpunt Ongebruikelijk Transacties
Den Haag: The Dutch Ministry of Justice, 2002

Moerland, H. and F. Boerman
Georganiseerde misdaad en betrokkenheid van bedrijven
Deventer: Gouda Quint, 1999

Nelen, H. and F. Lankhorst
Dilemmas facing the legal professions
(forthcoming)

Parlementaire Enquêtecommissie Opsporingsmethoden, Inzake opsporing
The Hague: Sdu, 1996

Passas, N. (ed.)
Transnational crime
Aldershot: Ashgate/Dartmouth, 1999

Regionaal Platform Criminaliteitsbeheersing Rotterdam, Regionaal Platform voor de Rotterdamse Haven en Industrie
Security Main port Rotterdam: een betrouwbare logistieke keten, Rotterdam:
Platform Criminaliteitbeheersing Rotterdam, 2000 (also available at
http://www.portofrotterdam.com) (dd. 29 April 2003)

Schaap, C.D.
Heling getoetst: studie naar witwassen van geld en de strafbaarstelling door
middel van de helingsbepalingen
Deventer: Gouda Quint, 1999

Schneider, S. M. Beare and J. Hill
Alternative Approaches to Combating Transnational Crime
Toronto: KPMG, 2000

Seger, A.
Preventive legal measures against organised crime
Strasbourg: Council of Europe, 2003

Sieber, U. and M. Bögel
Logistik der Organisierten Kriminalität
Wiesbaden: Bundeskriminalamt, 1993

Smith, D.
The Mafia mystique
New York: Basic Books, 1975

Struiksma, J. and F. Michiels
Gewapend bestuursecht
Zwolle: Tjeenk Willink, 1994

Terlouw, G.J. and U. Aron
Twee jaar MOT; een evaluatie van de Wet melding ongebruikelijke transacties
Arnhem: Gouda Quint, 1996

Transcrime
Euroshore; Protecting the EU financial system from the exploitation of financial
centres and offshore facilities by organised crime
Trento: University of Trento, 2000 (also see http://www.transcrime.unitn.it/
aree/progetti.dhtml?id=6) (dd. 16 October 2003)

Transcrime
Transparency and Money Laundering
Trento: University of Trento, 2001 (also see http://www.transcrime.unitn.it/
aree/progetti.dhtml?id=6) (dd. 16 October 2003)

White, S. (ed.)
Procurement and Organised crime; an EU-Wide Study
London: Institute of Advanced Legal Studies, 2000

Internet resources

Bizzo
> http://www.bizzo.nl/PUBLICATIES/ARTIKELEN/pakkans.html (dd. 20 April 2003)

CGKR
> http://www.antiracisme.be (dd. 20 April 2003)

Financial Supervision
> http://www.rata.bof.fi/english/Faq/data/data_money_laundering.html (dd. 29 April 2003)

First Gov. for consumers
> http://www.consumer.gov/idtheft/reports/gao-d02830t.pdf (dd. 20 April 2003)

GWK MoneyGram Money Transfer
> http://www.gwk.nl/pr_ce.htm (dd. 29 April 2003)

Kocbank
> http://www.kocbank.com.tr (dd. 29 April 2003)

Ministry of Justice
> http://www.justitie.nl/pers/berichten/index.asp) (dd. 12 November 2003)

Port of Rotterdam
> http://www.portofrotterdam.com (dd. 24 April 2003)

UK Passport Service
> http://www.ukpa.gov.uk/_history (dd. 29 April 2003) and
> http://www.ukpa.gov.uk/downloads/ICT2.pdf (dd. 29 April 2003)

United States General Accounting Office (2002)
> 'Identity Fraud; Prevalence and Links to Alien Illegal Activities',
> http://www.consumer.gov/idtheft/reports/gao-d02830t.pdf (dd. 20 April 2003)

Western Union Money Transfer
> http://www.postkantoren.nl/website/topnav/main/postbank/moneytransfer.html (dd. 29 April 2003)

Western Union
> http://www.westernunion.com (dd. 29 April 2003)

Appendix 1
Falcone Research on the Prevention of Organised Crime Questionnaire

1 The Network and its Illegal Activities

1.1 The criminal network

Hierarchical or fluid
If a group or network has a pyramid-shaped structure, the roles rarely change. Moreover, the tasks tend to be distributed and carried out according to fixed patterns.

If an organised crime network has a more fluid structure, its composition may vary according to the roles and tasks of its members. A 'fluid' network tends to react more swiftly and pragmatically to changing opportunities in its social environment. This does not mean, however, that in more flexible networks no distribution of tasks takes place. A more detailed analysis of the distribution of roles will follow in section 2.

1.1.2 Composition
Who are members of the group? Include a description of the members' ethnicity and background. Also include, if possible, how and where they met each other.

1.2 Primary activities

Describe the type of activities undertaken by the criminal network. If necessary, include a reference to secondary activities (e.g. drug smuggling combined with the smuggling of weapons).

2 Modus operandi

2.1 Logistic roles of the members of organised crime networks

This part emphasises the distribution of tasks among the members of the organised crime network.

2.1.1 How are the tasks distributed among members of the network?

Who is responsible for carrying out certain tasks and why?

2.1.2 What are the specific roles and tasks of the prime suspects?

Focus on the most important persons in the criminal network.

2.1.3 Do the 'leaders' of the networks have exclusive contacts or exclusive qualities that are crucial to the network?

What are the reasons for the high status of the most important persons in the network? Do they have contacts (family relations) with key persons which are crucial to the illegal activities of the network? Or do they have characteristics that make them difficult to replace? For instance, do they have exclusive contacts with drug suppliers in Colombia, with the document forgers, airport personnel, police officers, etc.? The 'leaders' may also be unique because of their personalities and charisma.

2.2   Procurement (Supply or Acquisition) logistics

The term 'procurement' is used to designate the chain of activities needed in the preparatory stages.
The network has to establish contact with the suppliers of goods. They need to reflect on how the goods or persons will be smuggled. They have to organise means of transportation and choose (alternative) smuggling routes. The group also needs to recruit persons who will carry out the actual smuggling.
In addition, it is important to reflect on the ways in which the criminal network ensure there is a demand for their illegal goods or services. Who are their clients? How much do they have to pay for the illegal goods and services? (also see 2.4).

Examples:
a   *Drugs*: Describe how the network establishes contacts with the producers of drugs or the companies producing the precursors needed to make drugs. Describe the process of buying drugs or the ingredients for making them.
b   *Smuggling of human beings*: Making contact with persons who want to go to another country or who want their family members to go to another country. Establishing reliable contacts with smugglers (often each responsible for parts of the route). How are the smuggling routes and means of travel organised? How does the network secure safe passage across borders (e.g. by corruption or friendly connections at the borders) and safe entry into the EU or the country of destination?
c   *Trafficking of human beings*: Describe the process of recruiting and smuggling of trafficked persons. Start with the demand of sex industry and describe the contacts of the criminal network with local sex club owners. Describe the recruitment process. How does the network establish its contacts with recruiters and smugglers? How are the women/men/children recruited? Are they lured by false promises, such as making lots of money as prostitutes, getting well-paid jobs as waitresses, dancers, au pairs (etc.), or are they kidnapped?

2.3 Production logistics

With the term 'production' logistics, we refer to the actual illegal activities undertaken by the group, i.e. the production of drugs, the smuggling of drugs, and/or the ingredients needed to make them.

Even though it is rather difficult to speak of 'production' regarding the smuggling of/trafficking in persons, we will use the same term. In relation to these activities, we need to think of the activities undertaken to obtain documents needed to cross borders and the actual process of smuggling persons to the country of destination. What means of transportation are chosen by the criminal network? Are persons smuggled directly from country A to country E, or do they stop at B and D (safe houses)?

Examples:
a   *Drugs*: Describe the process of producing drugs, synthetic or otherwise (if the network produces the drugs themselves). Describe how the network organises the means and routes of transportation. How does the network try to ensure that the drugs enter the country of destination undetected by the authorities? How and where are the drugs stashed?
b   *Smuggling of human beings*: Describe the process of illegal immigration. How does the network obtain travel documents and visas, false or otherwise?
c   *Trafficking human beings*: See under (b) + How do the smugglers take control of the trafficked persons during the journey (for instance should the women become suspicious and want to go home)? Furthermore, women may be forced to work in transit countries.

For instance, in the Netherlands we have found that certain criminal networks traffic women from Central and Eastern Europe to the EU. In the EU, they have to work as prostitutes in Italy and Germany before they have to work in the Dutch sex industry.

2.4 Marketing logistics

With the term 'marketing' logistics, we refer to the process of advertising and selling illegal products or services.
Some criminal groups may use normal legal advertising methods, for instance, in the ethnic press. For selling their goods and services, reliable contacts with persons willing to pay for their goods and services are indispensable.
Criminal groups may also compete with other criminals by reducing the 'standard' prices for goods or services.
Prices may reflect the risks involved with supplying the illegal goods or services, or they may reflect the availability of the goods or services. For instance, smuggling illegal immigrants from Asia to the Netherlands is much cheaper than smuggling them from Asia to the United Kingdom. This is, *inter alia*, because of the fact that illegal immigrants smuggled by lorry to the UK are much easier to detect, since

the trucks all have to board ships/ferries departing from ports such as Calais to England. In addition, the UK as a country of destination is in great demand by, for instance, persons from Pakistan and China.

Examples:
a   *Drugs*: How does the network sell its drugs and to whom? Has the network established reliable contacts with dealers, intermediate or otherwise? What is the price of drugs supplied by the criminal network? Is it the same as other networks or do they compete with lower prices (to gain control over a certain market)? Do they use violence to obtain a share of the consumer market?
b   *Smuggling of human beings*: How does the network advertise its smuggling operation, both in the countries of origin and destination? What do they charge for smuggling? If possible, state the different prices for various parts of the smuggling route, e.g. Iran-Turkey: $500; Turkey-Albania: $1,000; Albania-Italy: $4,000; Italy/Belgium-England: $7,000.
c   *Trafficking human beings*: Describe the distribution channel. How does the network advertise its capacity to provide the sex industry with prostitutes? How does it secure a steady demand for prostitutes? Does the network work in close cooperation with owners of clubs or brothels and pimps, or does the network own brothels? If they own their own sex clubs or bars, how did they obtain commercial licenses to run it? Do they offer protection to the brothel owners (= their clients)?

Does the network use violence? (The intrusion of foreign criminal networks into a local market often goes hand in hand with violent confrontations with local networks).
Describe the strategies used to take control of the trafficked persons. How does the network (or how do the associated pimps) secure the presence of a sufficient number of prostitutes (low cost or otherwise) in their clubs (e.g. by the debt bondage of prostitutes, strategies to prevent detection of illegal prostitutes in the sex clubs by the police and the subsequent deportation of prostitutes)?

N.B. Marketing logistics are of greater importance regarding the trafficking in persons. In order to achieve a certain degree of stability in the chain of supply and demand, it is necessary for the range of women (men or children) offered to the sex industry to change constantly and maintain their attractiveness for their clients. In addition to regular customers, there are many undecided potential clients who roam the scene. The goal is to convince them.
Clearly, criminal groups active in the trafficking business need to cooperate with brothel owners and pimps to maximise profits and to do business on a supra-regional or international level.
Upon the arrival at the brothel, the prospective prostitutes must be placed under control and escape must be prevented. They are therefore told that they are deeply in debt to the criminal network and the pimps they have to work for. Frequently their passports are taken away from them. With no money and no

passports the trafficked persons have no hope of escape. In addition, due to language problems, mistrust of the police and fear for deportation, they do not easily turn to the authorities.

2.5 Financial logistics

2.5.1 Describe the network's profit estimates (selling prices minus costs)

For instance, with regard to the trafficking of human beings, the following estimate could be made:

Profits: 1 prostitute has an average of 5 clients per day, who pay an average of $50 for sex = $250 per day. Prostitutes work about 25 days per month = $6,250. The network exploits 10 prostitutes per month ($62,500). The network also sells prostitutes (e.g. after 3 months) to other networks for $3,000. Total average monthly proceeds: $62,500 + $9,000 (the proceeds of selling 3 persons to other networks).

Expenses: The recruitment and network of illegal entry costs $2,000 per trafficked person. The network traffics about 5 persons per month. Other expenses are, for instance, rent of the brothel ($750), the costs of food/clothes and lodging for prostitutes (per prostitute: $200 per month).
Average net monthly profits are thus $58,750 < ($62,500 +$9,000) – ($10,000+ $750+ $2000).

2.5.2 Describe how the network spends the proceeds of crime

For instance, whether and what part of the proceeds is spent on luxury goods and an expensive lifestyle (e.g. on cars, jewellery, wining and dining friends, parties, etc.)

2.5.3 Describe the network's investments

What parts of the proceeds are invested in real estate, businesses, etc.? How and where do they invest the proceeds?

2.5.4 Describe the networks' money laundering activities

Does the criminal network launder the proceeds? If so, who takes part of the actual laundering of the proceeds? How is it done and where? Is the laundering done abroad or at home? What companies/banks/currency exchange offices are involved?
Include any money laundering activities done by others on behalf of the network.

2.5.5 Does the network use underground banking?

Underground banking is also referred to as Hawala (Pakistan), Hundi (India), or Fei ch'ien (China).

The phenomenon of underground banking

Underground banking is a traditional way of banking amongst Asian (and African) people. It is predominantly based on trust. It probably dates from a time when official banks did not yet exist. Today, it is often used by ethnic minorities to send money home (i.e. to support their families). The advantage of underground banking is that it is swift and cheap. Moreover, money can be sent to the most remote areas, if the banker has a partner in that area.

The basic *modus operandi* is as follows: Clients approach underground bankers to request that a certain sum of money is transferred to country X. Bankers will call or fax the details to their associate in that country and payment will be made within hours to the recipient. In some cases, clients may wish to pick up the money themselves. If this is so, a code will be given to the client for reference to the underground banker in the country where the money will be picked up. This code is communicated to the banker responsible for the payment. The bankers profit comes from currency exchange rates manipulation and/or a commission. In most instances, money is transferred without actually moving the money. The accounts are balanced from time to time between the bankers through transfers via conventional bank routes, postal money orders, the smuggling of currency or through invoice manipulation. This can be done as follows: the banker in the Netherlands buys $150,000 worth of consumer goods, and sends these to India with an official invoice of only $70,000. The Indian banker retrieves $80,000 by selling the goods at a profit.

Underground banking is thus a system, or network of people, facilitating the transfer of money domestically or internationally *outside* the conventional, regulated financial systems, i.e. normal banks or money transfers systems (such as MoneyGram, Western Union). Underground banking is characterised by trust and underground bankers are often family members.

3   Contacts with the illicit environment

3.1   Contacts with other groups

3.2   Interactions with fellow criminals

3.2.1 Cooperation or competition

How is/are knowledge/expertise/manpower/illegal goods or services exchanged between different criminal networks?

3.2.2 The role of facilitators

Facilitators are persons who render specific services, such as document forgers, carriers, brokers, personal property agents, persons assisting in money laundering activities.

3.2.3 Territorial deals or disputes

The term 'territorial deals' refers to the situation where criminal groups have reached an agreement about who operates in what part of the market. Territorial disputes, on the other hand, are (violent) clashes between criminal groups about the right to sell their products or their services in a particular area.

3.2.4 Methods of concealment

Criminal networks may anticipate threats or competition from other networks. This may in return lead to the use of code languages and the concealment of activities, even from their fellow criminals

3.2.5 Violence

Does the network use acts of violence towards other networks? For instance, rip deals, threats, intimidation, liquidations, extortion, blackmail and/or kidnapping.

3.3 Interactions with terrorist or separatist groups

4 Contacts with the licit environment

4.1 Shielding against investigation and prosecution

In general, criminal groups tend to hide their activities from the authorities. This can be done by, for instance, screening members of the criminal network (e.g. to determine that there are no snitches or undercover agents) and by the destroying or falsifying the network's 'paper trail' and the use of code languages, etc. However, a group may also go much further and employ strategies which are aimed at attacking the criminal justice authorities. For instance, they may use counter surveillance (the group informs policemen that they know what cars they drive or where their wives work or children go to school). Other strategies may involve blackmail (e.g. obtaining compromising photographs of police officers or public prosecutors, etc.), intimidation, and/or the use of violence (excessive or otherwise) against police officers, prosecutors and magistrates.

4.2 Corruption

Describe the nature and extent of individual contacts with people working at the national or local government, law enforcement agencies, public prosecution departments, courts, customs and excise etc..

4.3 Contacts with facilitators

Describe the nature, extent and purpose of individual contacts with:
– Lawyers

- Tax advisors
- Stock brokers
- Real estate agents
- Accountants
- Notaries
- Other specialists

Such external experts or specialists may either actively or passively be cooperating with a criminal network.

The passive cooperation of facilitators exists when they deliberately disregard or pretend to disregard something. Real estate agents, for instance, may decide not to ask too many questions if a certain building is purchased with suitcases full of cash. A recent example in the Netherlands: a criminal network was able to buy a hotel in Amsterdam for $1 million cash; no questions were asked.

4.4   Interactions with legitimate businesses

What kind of relationships with licit and/or legal enterprises and entities have been established?

What is the nature and extent of the involvement of the licit environment in the criminal activities?

To what extent are the legal entities aware of the fact that they are involved in organised crime or are being subject to abuse by criminals?

Keep the following possibilities in mind:
- Businesses may be facilitating illegal activities directly (e.g. operating as a shell company or a smoke screen) or indirectly (by not asking too much questions)
- Businesses may render specific services (changing money, laundering money, underground banking and/or informal value transfer systems, falsifying documents, transport goods or people, supply corporate bodies)
- Businesses may provide criminals a place to meet or to stay.

1.5   Opportunities for prevention

What facilitated or hindered the offenders in performing their illegal activities and what barriers can be put up against these activities?

For instance:
- Isolate weaknesses or potential weaknesses in the chain of contacts between criminals.
- Address factors which are conducive to crime in public policy, such as the lack of checks or surveillance; low priority given to certain types of investigation; gaps in laws and regulations, etc.);

(*Example*: In the Netherlands, there are too few incentives for airline companies to check the validity of passengers' documents. Illegal immigrants are also known to bypass gate checks at airports with the assistance of airport personnel. Airports do not seem to use thorough checks when employing personnel handling suitcases and cargo.)

- Preventive measures regarding contacts with the legitimate environment (*Example*: In the Netherlands, cases involving the smuggling of illegal immigrants reveal that visas were not only obtained by corruption but also through fake letters of invitation by European companies. Pre-boarding checks seemed to deter the smugglers of illegal immigrants. However, this may lead criminals to use smaller, regional airports with less strict surveillance. The level of surveillance at small, regional airports must be therefore brought up to the standards of international airports.)

Appendix 2
Opportunities detected
in the national reports

'Red flags'

ILLICIT ENVIRONMENT

a. The demand for illegal products and services

Italy	Black labour and street prostitution.
The Netherlands	Illegal products and services, and in particular the smuggling of human beings and the trafficking of women.

b. Criminal contacts

Finland	Ethnic minorities.
	Prisons as facilitators.
Hungary	Falsifiers of official documents.
Italy	Cooperation between criminal groups.
	Illegal facilitators, the workforce, micro-criminals, socially excluded people.
	Easiness of deceiving victims.
The Netherlands	Handymen.
	Facilitators.
	Bridge builders.
	Underground bankers.

c. Violence

Hungary	Intimidation of witnesses.
Italy	Firearms.
	Violence to protect own network.

d. Information, communication and documents

Finland	Information technology and communication.
Hungary	Shielding using false documents.
Italy	See the remark on the abuse of official documents in the licit environment.
The Netherlands	The availability of stolen documents and materials, such as copper stamps and watermarks, necessary to authenticate forged documents.

e. Front store activities

The Netherlands	Organised crime groups set up businesses merely to facilitate their illegal activities.

LICIT ENVIRONMENT

a. Abuse of officials or corruption

Hungary	Suspicion of corruption (not only in the 15 cases described in the report, but in earlier cases corruption had also been detected).
Italy	Corruption of law enforcement agents, in particular, in East Europe.
The Netherlands	Corruption or misleading officials particularly on a local level concerning the prostitution branch.

b. Abuse of official and informal financial services

Finland	Business activities for money laundering.
Hungary	Suspicion of money laundering.
Italy	Financial banking system.
	Non-traditional financial channels.

The Netherlands	Financial institutes in other countries.
	Certain 'extra' services by nontraditional financial institutes, such as MoneyGram.

c. Abuse of professions

Italy	Legal professions: the role of lawyers, notaries, auditors, accountants, tax consultants in criminal networks.
The Netherlands	Legal professions: in particular lawyers and legal advisors.

d. Abuse of legal facilitators

Finland	People who provide premises for criminal activities.
Hungary	Owners of safe houses, connections with taxi drivers or car rental services.
Italy	Legal facilitators, such as hotel owners, landlords, taxi drivers.
The Netherlands	See abuse of commercial businesses.

e. Abuse of legal commercial activities

Finland	Business activities, such as transport and garage business, and the catering and entertainment business.
Hungary	Suspicion of connections with travel agencies.
Italy	Infiltration in legal commercial activities (commercial entrepreneurs with a criminal background).
The Netherlands	Many individuals in the world of legitimate business are willing to ignore or tolerate obvious criminal activities or even to profit from them as long as the risks involved seem minor.

f. Abuse of official documents

Hungary	It is to easy to use false Hungarian passports at foreign borders.
Italy	It is to easy to falsify identification documents.
The Netherlands	It is easy to forge documents and the trade in these documents is extensive.

g. Lack of criminal legislation and regulation

Hungary	Lack of tough sanctions.
Italy	Lack of criminal legislation against smuggling and trafficking in some EU countries.
	The trafficking of women is not a specific offence in the Italian criminal code, but this behaviour is punished by being treated as a series of other criminal offences. The lack of simplicity could be an obstacle.
The Netherlands	Inadequacies in the legislation on smuggling human beings, so that staying in or leaving of the Netherlands cannot be punished.
	Possible facilitating aspects or negative effects of condoning policy.
	The asylum procedure is subject to abuse by criminal groups for smuggling or trafficking people to the Netherlands.

h. Lack of law enforcement and surveillance

Hungary	There is not enough invested in law enforcement.
Italy	Lack of effective checks in field of black labour.
The Netherlands	Border checks.
	Condoning policy.
	The sub-letting of accommodation

Appendix 3
Preventive measures presented
in the national reports

Preventive measures

ILLICIT ENVIRONMENT

---

a. The demand for illegal products and services

Italy	Structural measures in labour market on a local level and aimed at discriminated categories of people, so they cannot be recruited by organised crime.
	Safeguard the weak elements in prostitution, i.e. the trafficked woman, not necessary to regulate the market of prostitution.
The Netherlands	Better surveillance of the employment of illegal immigrants, especially in businesses or branches in which criminal groups invest on local level, and connecting different important databases for the effective exchange of information.

b. Criminal contacts

Finland	Making a proper risk analysis.
	Using effective preventive integration programmes.
	Make the pre-arrival training in Estonia and Russia more adequate (it currently appears to be inadequate).
	No longer underestimate the complexity of the integration process.
	Regarding prisons: the contact between fellow prisoners should be restricted as well as that with the outside world of organised and professional crime e.g. by means of location and, for example, in Finland the discussion has also emerged about the possible reallocation of drugs barons by means of a kind of segregation.
Italy	Stronger international cooperation amongst police authorities in creating obstacles and risks in the links between perpetrators.
	Involvement of victims in helping the police and justice system to detect and prosecute criminals by reporting their cases to the police for which they would be rewarded with certain advantages.
	Increase the police force.
	Legal definition of 'trafficking in human beings' and increase sanctions.
	Reducing conditions of exclusion and marginality.
	Provide information to potential victims or people in countries of origin about the possibilities and limitations of legal immigration and about the risks and exploitation related to the illegal services of traffickers.
The Netherlands	The investigative authorities should focus on the 'bridge builders' because they are often the 'leaders' or decision makers of the criminal groups.
	The investigative authorities should also focus on the facilitators, such as forgers and underground bankers as they facilitate the criminal activities of several crime groups.
	Regarding the underground bankers: it should be investigated whether it would be advisable to impose regulations such as the money laundering measures to reduce their services for organised crime groups.

c. Violence

Hungary	Witness protection is included in the criminal code in Hungary (1998) but so far it has failed to fulfil the expectations.
Italy	Make the supply of firearms more difficult to reduce violence.
	Policies to reduce violence.

d. Information, communication and documents

Finland	A Government Bill that makes it possible to wiretap the phone instead of monitoring subscriptions (IMEI code, expected to be adopted by the Parliament in spring 2002).
	Measures to correct police practice (better searching methods).
	Finland has the right to deny the use of encoded messages which had been high on the political agenda but it would seems to be impossible to deny this right only on the basis of law enforcement purposes.
Hungary	The falsifying of documents has to be made more difficult.
Italy	Making documents foolproof to reduce the possibility of falsifying.
The Netherlands	More attention should be paid to the security in places where passports are stored, e.g. town halls.
	The original materials used to make documents official, such as copper stamps and watermarks, should also be subjected to greater security measure.
	The forging of documents should be made more difficult.

e. Front stores

The Netherlands	It should be possible to screen people who want to set up or take over companies, whereby the screening authority should pay attention to the possible use of straw men.

LICIT ENVIRONMENT

a. Abuse of officials or corruption

Hungary	The integrity of public and business life has to be increased.
	Wide-scale investigations should be carried out into the properties and financial situations of people who work in the public sphere and those working in crime management and crime detection.
Italy	Anti-corruption measures have to be adopted.
	More effective checks should take place of all people involved in the public and private sectors.
The Netherlands	In all circumstances, governmental authorities should be alert for possible corruption, codes of conduct should be established and personnel should be screened.

b. Abuse of traditional and non-traditional financial institutes

Finland	Finland has made the reporting of suspicious money transfers obligatory.
Hungary	Money laundering was included in the Hungarian Criminal Code in 1994, but so far no convictions have taken place. Money and time should be made available to execute financial investigations and the courts should order such investigations.
Italy	Banks should be more careful and suspicious about financial operations (e.g. so-called "smurfing", networks) as indicators that illegal activities are being performed
	More control should be imposed on the services of nontraditional financial institutes.
The Netherlands	Other countries should be stimulated to establish anti-money laundering measures.
	International cooperation with regard to financial investigations should be improved.
	'Extra' services, such as MoneyGram, should be made less attractive.

c. Abuse of professions

Finland
Increase the awareness of criminal intentions among real estate agents and social welfare agencies.
Indicate the importance of maintaining the quality and reputation of a neighbourhood.
Prevent neighbourhoods from falling into decay and ensure they remain attractive to the well-behaved residential population.
More effective surveillance on the actual use of social welfare services accommodation.
Increase information about the restrictions and related sanctions regarding the use of accommodation by third parties (according to the authors this would keep a number of potential facilitators out of the criminal market)

Italy
Develop strategies to shield professions from the infiltration of organised crime, making them less vulnerable.

The Netherlands
Further development of increasing the awareness and regulations concerning facilitating activities.

d. Abuse of legal facilitators

Finland
Increase the awareness of criminal intentions among real estate agents and social welfare agencies.
Indicate the importance of maintaining the quality and reputation of a neighbourhood.
Prevent neighbourhoods from falling into decay and ensure they remain attractive to the well-behaved residential population.
More effective surveillance on the actual use of social welfare services accommodation.
Increase information about the restrictions and related sanctions regarding the use of accommodation by third parties (according to the authors this would keep a number of potential facilitators out of the criminal market)

Hungary
Checks of transport facilitators should be increased.

Italy
Effective checks of the occupations mentioned should take place to avoid cooperation with organised crime groups.

The Netherlands
Checks should take place to avoid cooperation with all kinds of businesses.
Regarding subletting: landlords should be made aware of areas of possible abuse and public administration should execute checks.

e. Abuse of legal commercial activities

Finland
Only CCC has accepted prohibiting convicted offenders from engaging in business.
More attention should be paid to regulating business ownership, business deals and the qualifications for companies to do business.
The role of the Trade Register is crucial, changes in company ownership should be subject to strict and increasingly active checks to impede money laundering.
Role of auditors in relation to the Trade Register: companies should not be allowed to continue running their businesses and being enrolled in the Trade Register without timely and proper audits of financial statements and tax declarations taking place.
The personal liability of owners should be strengthened.
Business partners should be required to check the validity of Trade Register data.

The exchange of information concerning business companies are of considerable importance in implementing efficient and productive surveillance practices without an excessive growth in bureaucracy.

Increase the awareness of contractors about the possibility of malfeasance by their employees.

Surveillance of the employees.

Strengthen position of employees who refuse illegal commitments by the compensation of financial losses.

Financial sanctions should be imposed for using company staff or equipment for illegal purposes.

In cooperation with trade unions, search for solutions which would contribute to a more effective and frequent identification and reporting of criminal activities.

Execute similar border and custom checks for vessel personnel as exist for passengers.

No longer allow crews to bypass passport checks at airports.

Italy   Use a tool such as a monitoring system on specific economic activities.

The Netherlands   A screening system for setting up or taking over businesses should be further developed.

Codes of conduct and certification within various branches should be stimulated.

f. Abuse of official documents

Hungary   The falsifying of documents should be made more difficult.

Italy   Format the regulation of identity documents

More effective checks on the authenticity of identifying documents by using electronic surveillance systems.

Make the identification of false documents more easy.

In-flight checks.

The Netherlands   Regarding the crossing of borders with the required documents: the check on marriages of convenience should once again be increased; embassies should pay more attention to visa applications on the basis on invitations by companies and such companies should be investigated, and an effective detection system should be established for people who apply for new documents.

g. Lack of criminal legislation and regulation

Hungary   It is necessary to unify court practice and apply sanctions more consequently. The sanctions judges impose on human trafficking are generally not tough enough.

Italy   Further steps should be taken to harmonise criminal laws in the field of the EU and elsewhere.

The Netherlands   Adjust legislation where inadequacies have been detected in such way that it does not facilitate organised crime and it no longer makes necessary activities of law enforcement agencies impossible.

Centres for asylum seekers should improve their registration systems. These centres should report 'escapes' from the centres to the police and the exchange of information between the authorities involved should be improved.

h. Lack of law enforcement

Hungary   The surveillance activities of the authorities should be intensified.

Secret methods of detection and investigation should be developed for these types of crime.

	Certain other measures should also be taken: increasing staff, facilitating technological developments and improving the communication.
Italy	Establishing simple national mechanisms to improve the surveillance of the labour market could reduce criminal activities at an international level.
The Netherlands	Regarding the crossing of borders with forged documents: high-tech equipment should be made available and the number of personnel should increase. Checks should be extended to small airports as well.

De WODC-rapporten

Om zo veel mogelijk belanghebbenden te informeren over de onderzoeksresultaten van het WODC wordt een beperkte oplage van de rapporten kosteloos verspreid onder functionarissen, werkgroepen en instellingen binnen en buiten het ministerie van Justitie. Dit gebeurt aan de hand van een verzendlijst die afhankelijk van het onderwerp van het rapport opgesteld wordt. De rapporten in de reeks Onderzoek en beleid (O&B) worden uitgegeven door Boom Juridische uitgevers en zijn voor belang-stellenden die niet voor een kosteloos rapport in aanmerking komen, te bestellen bij Boom distributiecentrum, postbus 400, 7940 AK Meppel, tel.: 0522-23 75 55, via e-mail: bdc@bdc.boom.nl.
Een complete lijst van de WODC-rapporten is te vinden op de WODC-site (www.wodc.nl). Daar zijn ook de uitgebreide samenvattingen te vinden van alle vanaf 1997 verschenen WODC-rapporten. Volledige teksten van de rapporten (vanaf 1999) zullen met terugwerkende kracht op de WODC-site beschikbaar komen. Hieronder volgen de titelbeschrijvingen van de in 2001, 2002 en 2003 verschenen rapporten.

Huls, F.W.M., M.M. Schreuders, M.H. Ter Horst-van Breukelen, F.P. van Tulder (red.)
Criminaliteit en rechtshandhaving 2000; ontwikkelingen en samenhangen
2001, O&B 189

Jungmann, N., E. Niemeijer, M.J. ter Voert
Van schuld naar schone lei; evaluatie Wet Schuldsanering natuurlijke personen
2001, O&B 190

Leuw, Ed., N. Mertens
Evaluatie beginselenwet Tbs/wet Fokkens
2001, O&B 191

Huijbregts, G.L.A.M., F.P van Tulder, D.E.G. Moolenaar
Model van justitiële jeugdvoorzieningen voor prognose en capaciteit
2001, O&B 192

Kruissink, M., C. Verwers
Het nieuwe jeugdstrafrecht; vijf jaar ervaring in de praktijk
2001, O&B 193

Verrest, P.A.M.
Ter vergelijking; een studie naar het Franse vooronderzoek in strafzaken
2001, O&B 194

Kamphorst, P.A., G.J. Terlouw
Van vast naar mobiel; een evaluatie van het experiment met elektronisch huisarrest voor minderjarigen als modaliteit voor de voorlopige hechtenis
2002, O&B 195

Moolenaar, D.E.G., F.P. van Tulder, G.L.A.M. Huijbregts, W. van der Heide
Prognose van de sanctiecapaciteit tot en met 2006
2002, O&B 196

Bokhorst, R.J., C.H. de Kogel, C.F.M. van der Meij
Evaluatie van de Wet BOB; fase 1: de eerste praktijkervaringen met de Wet bijzondere opsporingsbevoegdheden
2002, O&B 197

Kleemans, E.R., M.E.I. Brienen, H.G. van de Bunt m.m.v. R.F. Kouwenberg,
G. Paulides, J. Barendsen
Georganiseerde criminaliteit in Nederland; tweede rapportage op basis van de
WODC-monitor
2002, O&B 198

Voert, M. ter, J. Kuppens
Schijn van partijdigheid rechters
2002, O&B 199

Daalder, A.L.
Het bordeelverbod opgeheven; prostitutie in 2000-2001
2002, O&B 200

Klijn, A.
Naamrecht
2002, O&B 201

Kruissink, M., C. Verwers
Jeugdreclassering in de praktijk
2002, O&B 202

Eshuis, R.J.J.
Van rechtbank naar kanton; evaluatie van de competentiegrensverhoging voor
civiele handelszaken in 1999
2002, O&B 203

Meijer, R.F., M. Grapendaal, M.M.J. van Ooyen, B.S.J. Wartna, M. Brouwers,
A.A.M. Essers
Geregistreerde drugcriminaliteit in cijfers; achtergrondstudie bij het
Justitieonderdeel van de Nationale Drugmonitor: Jaarbericht 2002
2003, O&B 204

Tak, P.J.J.
The Dutch criminal justice system; organization and operation – second revized
edition
2003, O&B 205

Kromhout, M., M. van San
Schimmige werelden; nieuwe etnische groepen en jeugdcriminaliteit
2003, O&B 206

Kogel, C.H. de, C. Verwers
De longstay afdeling van Veldzicht; een evaluatie
2003, O&B 207

Moolenaar, D.E.G., G.L.A.M. Huijbregts
Sanctiecapaciteit 2007; een beleidsneutrale prognose
2003, O&B 208

Eshuis, R.J.J.
Claims bij de rechtbank
2003, O&B 209

Combrink-Kuiters, L., E. Niemeyer, M. ter Voert m.m.v. N. Dijkhoff,
M. van Gammeren-Zoeteweij, J. Kuppens
Ruimte voor Mediation
2003, O&B 210
Heide, W. van der, A.Th.J. Eggen (red.)
Criminaliteit en rechtshandhaving 2001; Ontwikkelingen en samenhangen
2003, O&B 211
European Sourcebook
European Sourcebook of Crime and Criminal Justice Statistics – 2003
2003, O&B 212
Smit, P.R., F.P. van Tulder, R.F. Meijer, P.P.J. Groen
Het ophelderingspercentage nader beschouwd
2003, O&B 213
Dijksterhuis, B.M., M.J.G. Jacobs, W.M. de Jongste
De competentiegrens van enkelvoudige kamers in strafzaken
2003, O&B 214
Bunt, H.G. van de, C.R.A. van der Schroot
Prevention of Organised Crime
2003, O&B 215